Stare at Me

How Being Blindsided Brings Life Into Focus

JOEY MULLANEY

with Michele Matrisciani

Library of Congress Cataloging-in-Publication Data
Names: Mullaney, Joey, 1994- author. | Matrisciani, Michele, author.
Title: Stare at me : how being blindsided brings life into focus / Joey Mullaney with Michele Matrisciani.
Description: First. | Georgetown, Ohio : KiCam Projects, [2021]
Identifiers: LCCN 2021010492 (print) | LCCN 2021010493 (ebook)
ISBN 9781734564235 (paperback) | ISBN 9781734564242 (epub)
Subjects: LCSH: Mullaney, Joey, 1994—Health. | Friedreich's ataxia—Patients—Biography. | Friedreich's ataxia—Patients—Massachusetts—Biography. | Adjustment (Psychology) | Breast—Cancer—Patients—-Massachusetts
Classification: LCC RC406.F7 M85 2021 (print) | LCC RC406.F7 (ebook)
DDC 616.8/30092 [B]—dc23
LC record available at https://lccn.loc.gov/2021010492
LC ebook record available at https://lccn.loc.gov/2021010493

Cover and book design by Mark Sullivan
Cover photography by Rachel Hogan

ISBN 978-1-7345642-3-5 (paperback)
ISBN 978-1-7345642-4-2 (ebook)
Printed in the United States of America

Published by KiCam Projects
Georgetown, Ohio

www.KiCamProjects.com

DEDICATION

To those who have picked me up whenever I have fallen,
literally and figuratively, thank you.

CONTENTS

I Like Dreaming

I like dreaming. I could do it all day and all night. I sometimes dream about asking a certain girl out on a date—and miraculously, she says yes. While falling asleep as I ride the T to my apartment after a long day in grad school, my mind wanders to what it might feel like to get an A on the paper I just turned in. When groggily eating breakfast, I fantasize about being in front of a sold-out crowd at Madison Square Garden, giving a motivational speech and receiving a standing ovation.

But the dreams I love most occur overnight when I am in a deep sleep; I can't tell the difference between dream and reality. The details from my subconscious are vivid, the images crystal clear.

One dream recurs every winter. It goes like this: I'm an NFL rookie wide receiver on my favorite team, the New England Patriots. It is the Super Bowl. We are down by five points with only sixty seconds left on the clock. The Seattle Seahawks have punted, so we have the ball. As I look to the Seattle sideline, I see a few of their players hanging out with the guy from the "My Pillow" infomercial, who is handing out two-for-one samples "FOR THIS ONE-TIME-ONLY DEAL!"

I hope this means Seattle is tired and out of plays. Suddenly my team has the ball in the red zone. In the New England huddle, the fearless Tom Brady (TB12) moves to call the final play. I share my intel about their defense with my teammate, Rob Gronkowski. "Gronk, the Seahawks have gone to sleep." (Genius observation by me.)

"We GOT this!" Gronk responds fiercely.

Brady calls the play and breaks the huddle. "Ready!" We grunt, clap, and ... "Break!"

Before I run out, Brady puts his palm to my chest to stop me. "The ball is coming to *you*, Joe. Be ready." I feel my heartbeat in my throat as we make our formation.

Somewhere on my journey from the huddle to the line of scrimmage, I realize that while I desperately wanted to be on the New England Patriots, I now feel the pressure of making a season-changing play! Brady hikes the ball, when suddenly I'm in my middle school's basketball gym.

I'm a seventh-grader playing in an intense basketball game. I'm at the free-throw line. I have one free throw left to win the game, but my arms will not lift. The Starbucks barista who saw me spill hot chocolate all over my uniform right before the game is one of the cheerleaders! Bill Belichick, wearing a cutoff sweatshirt with his hoodie up, is spotting the cheerleader/barista for a mid-air stunt, as they lead the crowd in a chant: "Smokin' Joe! Smokin' Joe! Smokin' Joe!"

Hearing the nickname my uncle gave me, I feel silly and slightly exposed wearing my gold-and-purple St. Anna's basketball jersey, stained with coffee. The bleachers are a cornucopia of the randomness of my life, including my two dogs, Aria and Duke; the mailman; my first-grade teacher; my mom; and Wiz Khalifa.

I'm still at the free-throw line. As I shoot the basketball, the hoop shifts and the basketball mutates into a spinning football. I'm suddenly back on the football field. I'm still Smokin' Joe but now wearing pads on the gridiron. The pressure comes back to me. Jimmy Fallon is defending me, and I want to ask him where he got his suit, but Brady snaps the ball, and I have to get moving.

I run three yards straight, then slant and lose Fallon. As TB12 releases the ball in my direction, the safety, Dwight Schrute from *The Office,* runs toward me. He won't be able to get me. I extend my arms to make the big catch and feel the cold pigskin tap my fingers.

I wake up.

I'm winded. Even though I'm lying in my bed, I'm out of breath. I feel pretty good, though, because I'm lying next to my supermodel wife in our king-sized bed. My body feels the fatigue of my exhilarating athletic feats. My muscles are sore, but still I muster the strength to roll over and get out of bed, even with the knot in my hamstring and my aching shoulder. I'm late for my much-needed postgame massage and sauna, and my head is pounding from the hangover of a celebratory locker-room champagne binge. I'm still elated, especially since my heroics made Coach Belichick smile.

And then I wake up. No, this time, I'm really awake, in my bedroom. I'm positive this is reality, because as I lift myself out of bed, I can't really move a muscle from my hips to my toes. Out of the corner of my eye, I see my scooter, in its usual spot, ready to take me to the bathroom. I begin the process of transferring myself from my bed to the scooter, where I will sit for the rest of my awake time.

I like dreaming.

PART ONE
Ordinary World

CHAPTER 1

Division I-Bound

The Mullaneys of Leominster, Massachusetts, grew up playing sports and idolizing athletes. Most kids align with their families' interests and mimic the things their parents and siblings do. There were the kids whose parents took them to New York City to see Broadway shows over winter break in grade school. Others traveled to Europe because their parents had wanderlust and enjoyed seeing the world. There were the science-focused families who saved up to visit landmarks like the space shuttle at Cape Canaveral. Some families were passionate about music, played instruments together, and went to many PG-rated outdoor concerts in the summers. My family loved sports—the more competitive, the better.

My father was athletic and played basketball. Since he only grew to about five feet eight, his playing days ended once he graduated high school. My mother, who is as tall as my dad, was also athletic. She ran track and played catcher for her high school softball team. After meeting in high school and eventually getting hitched, my mom and dad had four children: the oldest, Ryan, a three-sport athlete; Kaela, the only daughter, a dancer; and then the first set of twins in many generations, me and Sean. I purposely put myself third in the lineup since I am older than my twin brother by TWO WHOLE MINUTES, and in twin world, that's a big deal.

As a child, I would always think about what it would be like to do other extracurriculars, like art, music, travel, and science.

Being well-rounded seemed fantastic. When I grew up, well-rounded looked like switching our attention from Final Four basketball games to Red Sox spring training games. I learned how to rough up an opponent when carrying a football before I could do long division.

For example, during a recess football game in first grade, I ran for a touchdown against a team of second-graders. When I next had the ball, a second-grader named Jimmy T. tried to stop me from scoring. I stiff-armed him and accidentally gave him a bloody nose. Jimmy T. cried and bled *a lot*. He told his teacher, who sent me to the principal. My punishment included no recess for two days. I also had to write apology letters to Jimmy T. and my principal, saying how rude my actions were.

Thanks, Jimmy T. Football is a contact sport, so I hope your nose is crooked.

I also had rambunctious cousins who lived nearby. We were very close and had similar mindsets. Playing in my backyard often felt like survival of the fittest. Thankfully, Sean and I were larger than most other kids our age. We used that to our advantage back then. People knew us as "The Mullaney Twins."

I come from a close family. My mom and dad have three siblings apiece. There are ten grandkids on my mom's side, and on my father's side, nine. It was great growing up with so many cousins nearby. All my cousins' houses had lawns trampled on from backyard sports. My two older female cousins and Kaela were competitive dancers. From hip hop to jazz to ballet, they did it all. Sean and I went to more dance competitions than most Dance Moms. Whether it was practice, a recital, or a performance on a cruise ship, Sean and I suffered through. Some nights, when the older girl cousins babysat Sean and me, the girls would not feed us dinner until we both wore leotards and perfected one of their dance routines.

There is one beneficial aspect of being in a sports family: dedication to getting better. And I was dedicated. Ted Williams, who was arguably the best hitter known to man, was obsessed with perfecting his swing. He spent all his waking time with his bat, and he became great because he did nothing else. My grandpa was a diehard fan of his and taught me how to swing like "Teddy Ballgame." My grandpa told me everything he knew about him. One time, I told my grandpa that he looked like Ted Williams, and he gave me the biggest hug and kiss and thanked me profusely, as if I'd given him the winning lottery ticket. I played whatever sport I could with whoever was hanging in my neighborhood. I emulated Ted Williams' dedication and tried to practice all the time.

I had sharp reflexes and outrageous goals, like being able to shoot a basketball like Kobe Bryant, throw a football like Tom Brady, and catch a baseball like Ken Griffey Jr. I was tough, athletic, and willing to do whatever it took to win.

Okay, so maybe it sounds like I was a first-round draft pick. I wasn't. But when you are a young kid, this kind of stuff is life itself, and your imagination can become reality if the pieces fall into place.

Being a sports kid doesn't make you a dumb jock. Sports made me mentally sharper for other parts of life. Sports taught me about patience and teamwork. In basketball, missing deep shots forces you to focus, pass the ball, and sometimes get closer to the hoop. I learned to be patient, find my shot, and share the ball. We all want to be high scorers, but I had to be patient.

Your time will come, Joe. Just wait.

During summers and falls in elementary school, I played Pop Warner football for my city's team. Grueling football practices on hot summer nights will stay with me forever. Games made all those practices worth it. One game sticks out. I will always remember playing against Worcester (pronounced Wistaahhh by New Englanders), one of our rivals. Well, we viewed them as rivals, but they probably didn't see it that way—they always beat us. Every. Single. Time. Our coaches did a great job preparing us for this game by making us believe the rivalry was precisely like the Red Sox vs. Yankees, Celtics vs. Lakers, and the Patriots vs. … well, all NFL teams. We went into that game pumped. Our perspectives changed. We wanted to destroy them. Coach started me at defensive end. Defensive end is the position of superstars like Chase Young, Joey Bosa, and J.J. Watt and is one of the few positions that matter in Pop Warner football.

All season long, I avoided the trap most other defensive players fall into: simply tackling the ball carrier. Tackling is good, no doubt. It's a necessary part of playing defense and getting stops. But I figured, why only tackle the ball carrier when I could also take the ball from him? My entire mission as a defensive end was to stop the ball carrier and strip the ball clean. I loved getting stops and forcing turnovers, which would allow Sean, an offensive player, to enter the game. Sean played running back because he was big and quick.

Pop Warner teams rarely throw the ball; they run ninety percent of the time. I knew that, so I anticipated a run every play. When the opposing team called hike, I would shimmy around the opponent's failed attempt at blocking me. Then, I knew the opposing team's running back would expect a tackle or collision. That's when I would attack and force him to lose control of the ball and fumble. I got pretty good at it, and my coaches loved it when I succeeded, so our offense could score.

Despite the weeklong pump-up speeches by our coaches, gameday arrived, and we seemed outmatched yet again by "Wistaahhh." I thought we were going to lose by a lot. But to my surprise, our coaches were right. We could actually make this a competitive game. I finished with many tackles and four forced fumbles because I was like a pit bull harassing the mailman. Sean scored three touchdowns that game, which ended in a tie. That was annoying. Nobody wants a tie, but it was better than getting crushed.

Football season always ended at Thanksgiving, which was fine because it was getting cold and we could then shift to basketball. I played basketball for two separate teams: my city's travel team and my school's team, the St. Anna Tigers. Being on the travel team was considered good, and traveling to different towns to play other teams was an incredible experience. Multiple teams— see how well-rounded I am!

St. Anna's played on Saturday mornings, and the travel team played on Sundays. Weekends were filled with basketball. It was better than dance recitals. Because we had weekends filled with sports, we did not have to watch boring ballet! Being a real sports family means you fully commit. If you join the team, you play for the whole season, period.

Playing sports was more than just playing games. It was social. My teammates included my four best friends: Sean, my cousin Petey, Rocco, and Joey G. Everyone, even our parents, called us Joey M. and Joey G., just to make sure we all knew who was who. Looking back, my teams had an unfair advantage because all five of us were solid athletes. In sixth grade, we beat one team by forty points! We felt like the 2017-18 Golden State Warriors, an unfair matchup to most of the competition. I listened to music on my iPod while wearing baggy sweatpants with Timberland boots to every game. Then, I shot from wherever I was open like Steph Curry.

The basketball season would end with the brutal Boston winter. Warmer weather meant baseball season, and Little League was where Sean and I shone brightest. We were physically bigger for our age, so we felt like men among boys. Sean played shortstop and batted third. I played catcher and batted cleanup. It is a compliment to bat third and fourth because it means you have an excellent on-base average and can hit bombs. Teammates would cringe if they heard their names move from the top four to sixth or seventh. It was a demotion. One of my teammates threw his bat over the dugout fence when our coach moved him from second to eighth. That's what happens when you can't seem to pull yourself out of a three-game slump. You either give up, or you work yourself back up the batting order.

I did not know much about playing catcher, but since I was a big, athletic kid and knew how to catch and throw, my coach put me there. My older cousin Kevin came over after school one day and taught me how to play the position. Kevin was the starting catcher for his high school team and had played that position all his life. After every pitch was thrown, he advised me to catch the ball, whether ball or strike, and immediately move my mitt to the middle of the strike zone—a concept known as framing. Since the mitt is the target you give the pitcher, being strategic about where you put the target can help him. I decided to try this technique in my next game.

No matter where I caught the ball in the next game, my mitt always ended up right in the strike zone. After the first inning of catching, my coach put his arm around my shoulder and said, "Joey, great job! Where did you learn to frame the ball?" I was confused and just said, "Frame? You noticed? My older cousin taught me." Turns out, *all* catchers above twelve years old frame the ball to fool the umpire into believing the pitch was a strike. (I discovered framing the ball worked much more often than trying to disrupt a batter by telling him dumb *yo' mama* jokes.)

I felt essential playing catcher. It's the most utilized position in baseball. You're in on every play on defense; you cannot lose focus for one second. You learn to silently communicate with a pitcher, to help him develop his system.

As catcher, you're the only player on your team facing the field. I had the advantage of seeing everything—all the positions, all the players, all the plays necessary—and developed a keen eye for defensive strategy. I paid attention; I was dedicated.

Besides noticing how to frame a pitch or force a fumble in football, I began to see more things outside of sports. Teachers called me observant. I liked that. I didn't know it at the time, but one day, that skill would change the way I played the most significant game I would ever play: life.

CHAPTER 2

Trapped in My Head

For as long as I can remember, on the very first day of school, I started a countdown to summer. My parents never understood that even in elementary school, every minute of the day was spent learning, working.

It would kill me when adults would tell me how lucky I was to be a kid. *Huh, what did they know?* They grew up in olden times and did not have to worry about state exams, pop quizzes, or how fast you could type on a keyboard.

By the time June rolled around, my buddies and I all began to see the light at the end of the tunnel, and that light was shining bright on a kid's best dream: summer vacation. I planned to meet up with my buddies every day and double down on my football skills.

I grew up in a neighborhood where nine homes lined both sides of a street that ended at a circle. Collectively, there were twenty-four kids of all ages on the block. Luckily for Sean and me, nine of those kids were in our age range. We nine kids referred to ourselves as the Circle Mob, which younger me thought was cool but current me thinks is pretty odd.

Whenever it was nice out, we all played backyard sports together at one of the houses, and when it was snowy and cold, we all went sledding. We must have rung one another's doorbells more than 200 times over our childhood years, to ask if we could play. I can tell countless stories about when the Circle Mob would play manhunt and forget to find someone, or when I acciden-tally swung and lost grip of my brand-new Wiffle ball bat, hitting Steph's face and giving her a black eye. Or when Sean passed a ball to Bradley during a backyard basketball game and broke his index finger. Or when Franky's family lost their dog and the whole neighborhood went on a hunt to find him—and succeeded!

When I was ten, as we were inching closer to summer break, I woke one morning before dawn with an intense, burning pain in my left foot. The whole house was dark and everyone was asleep, so I stayed in bed and tried to swallow my cries, grabbing my foot to reduce the pain. It had been annoying me for the last few days, but I hadn't mentioned anything to anyone. Now I was in full-on pain, the kind of injury that feels like someone put a blow torch to your skin. I began to cry out until I got hysterical.

I tried moving around quietly to avoid waking my siblings in their rooms next door. But Sean shared a room with me, and he woke up. Before he could yell at me, I'd already decided to get out of bed and go downstairs.

I was met at the foot of the stairs by our dog, Max. He was not a friendly dog. In fact, many times, we considered getting a priest to perform an exorcism on Max. (However, we threw out that option so no priests would be harmed!) It was surprising that Max let me hug him while I lay on the kitchen floor and cried over my stinking foot. Max, a white, fluffy, fifteen-pound Lhasa Apso, was very territorial over my family, grandparents, and home. During his fourteen-year life, Max would not allow anybody to come in or out of our house without taking his pound of flesh. (Thankfully, nobody sued us.) Sitting with Max helped take my mind off my foot until morning, when my parents drove me to the hospital.

Because I'm part of a family that loves sports, being in the emergency room was no big deal when I was a kid. Stitches, broken bones, concussions, and sprains were par for the course. Nothing fazed me about hospital emergency rooms, but this time felt different. I felt injured, not just hurt. This time, I knew something was off. The doctor took an X-ray and an MRI of my foot (been there, done that a million times) and discovered a cyst. Then, he informed me I would need to go under the knife to remove this abnormality. Surgery was fine with me if it meant making the pain stop.

When I woke up after my operation, I thought it was pretty cool to have a cast on my foot. Until the doctors dropped the bomb:

"Joey, you will not be able to put any weight or pressure on your foot if you want it to heal correctly. You'll need four weeks in a wheelchair and then four more weeks in a walking boot, probably through July and August."

C'mon! You're taking away my entire summer! This sucks!

I tried to stay mad so I wouldn't break down and cry, but the thought of being confined to a wheelchair all summer long made the tears well up.

Being in a cast comes with many stupid rules: no sweating, no swimming, and no getting your cast wet in the shower. Let me tell you, dangling your leg outside of a shower door while cleaning your body is challenging. All I could do was sit inside and watch TV or play video games all summer. Although it could have been much worse, it sucked sitting inside watching my family, the Circle Mob, and all my cousins enjoy the short-lived ninety-five-degree summer days. One sunny afternoon when my cousins were swimming and playing endless games of Marco Polo and sharks and dolphins in my pool, I enviously stared at them through the window. I'd just finished playing my seventh consecutive game of NBA 2K4. I sat alone with silent tears streaming down my cheeks, so nobody saw me upset—especially my sister, Kaela.

When Kaela was around eight and I was almost four, her dance teacher noticed Kaela appeared to be off balance on her turns. The teacher thought the problem might be a symptom of an ear infection and suggested that our mom take Kaela to get her ears checked.

After learning she didn't have an ear infection but gaining no clarity on her balance issues, Kaela and my parents traveled to various doctors to figure out what was going on. A year passed before Kaela was diagnosed with a rare, debilitating, degenerative neuromuscular disease called Friedreich's ataxia (FA), as confirmed when Kaela went to Canada and met with the doctor who actually discovered the FA gene. At the time, even he didn't know much about FA—much less how to explain it to a child. He told Kaela and my parents it would be many years before Kaela's physical function would be greatly impacted. But in fact, it would be only two.

Kaela's physical difficulties increased quickly, and so did her worry and confusion about what was happening with her body. Finally, during a visit with an ataxia specialist in Boston, eleven-year-old Kaela looked at him and directly asked, "What's wrong with me?"

Kaela and my parents researched FA anywhere and everywhere they could. They learned that the disease would progressively destroy Kaela's hand-eye coordination and all of her nerves and muscles until she could no longer walk. They learned that FA eventually would give her a heart condition, erratic energy levels, speech complications, and diabetes—all the while threatening to shorten her life span by decades. And lastly, they learned that there was no cure or treatment.

By the summer I was in the wheelchair, six years after Kaela's diagnosis, my sister was still walking, though not well. She made FA look easy-peasy through her pain and discomfort, although I knew it was not. I couldn't understand how she could act so normal. Being in a wheelchair made me, for the first time, wonder how Kaela managed to live her life.

I would go with my parents and Kaela to her doctor visits and then from hospital to hospital, each more significant and more specialized than the last. I'm not talking about a small pediatrician's office with one receptionist and a lollipop jar. These were big Boston hospitals that took up half the block. Hospitals with hundreds of doctors and nurses running around, pushing people in stretchers, with loud machines making all kinds of medical noises. While the doctor examined Kaela, the doctor's assistant checked my balance and coordination in the other room. I figured she could tell me how to improve my basketball game.

Eventually, Kaela's illness forced her to quit dance. And years later, once Kaela was using a motorized scooter full-time, my parents tricked out the house to make it accessible. They even had an elevator installed.

On that warm summer day watching my cousins swim in the pool while I was confined to a wheelchair nursing a foot injury, I vowed never to be confined to a wheelchair again until I was old and gray with glasses and wrinkles. I felt guilty because even though Kaela lived like this all the time, I could not wait for my foot to heal. This was the *worst summer ever!*

To pass the time, and because I was tired of playing video games every day, I wanted to do something new. While watching ESPN one day, I saw a short interview on one of my favorite basketball players, Kobe Bryant. He was asked about the strategies he would use before playing against a great team. Kobe based his approach to basketball on patience. One of the tactics that helped him develop that skill was learning to play chess. I was surprised! But then Kobe explained how the fundamentals of playing chess helped him develop into one of the greatest basketball players of all time by teaching him to use his mind as a weapon. Since most NBA players are tall, strong, and quick, Kobe felt he needed something more to stand out. *Boom. Sold. Time for me to learn chess.*

Slowly, I learned chess on the computer. I started by learning the pieces, their functions, and how to move them. Chess is a battle, and as I inched around the board trying to capture the pieces on the opposing side, I could see how the game could remind someone of basketball and football. A pawn, seemingly the weakest piece, can only move one spot. A knight can only move in L-shaped directions. Bishops must move diagonally, and rooks can only move straight up and down or left and right. The queen can do everything the other pieces can do, and finally, the king controls the entire board but can only move one spot in any direction. Since I only ever played chess on the computer, on beginner mode, I always won. Although I wanted to be a potent threat like a queen or silently dominant like a king, I felt smaller than a pawn that summer.

The foot injury kept me on the sideline from every cool thing, including my Little League baseball team, where I was once the star catcher who batted cleanup. That summer, they won the city championship, led by Sean and my cousin Michael. I just wanted to help them win. I got to watch my teammates celebrate by jumping into a huddle after the final out of the championship game. My coaches tried to wheel me out to celebrate on the outskirts of the huddle, but my tires couldn't roll over the grassy field. It was just another example of my misery that summer.

Being in a wheelchair sucked, and so did my attitude. I was frustrated by being immobile and having to watch everybody else live their lives. I had to watch fun experiences that were supposed to be *my* experiences as if they were a movie. All I could do during those annoying wheelchair days was tell myself to calm down and refocus, that my confinement was only temporary. It helped get me through those long months.

CHAPTER 3

The Rule Is There Are No Rules

I may have been an on-the-field leader in baseball, but when it came to basketball, Sean emerged as the star. He was a natural. No matter how much I practiced, I eventually realized I would never be as good as Sean. He was big, quick, and agile. Until that point in my life, having a twin always felt like a gift. Now, parents and classmates would stop Sean after games or in the hallways to compliment his performance. They would praise him for his thirty-point games, or his fifteen assists, or his game-saving rebound, or that time he made a half-court shot at the buzzer before halftime. As much as I loved my brother, it started to bother me. I felt invisible. It seemed as if nobody cared about my stats, even when I played well. I felt like when Sean was around, nobody noticed me.

My frustrations on the basketball court started to extend to other parts of my life, including my once-beloved baseball. At times, baseball seemed too slow-paced relative to basketball and football. My performance started to get worse the summer I was in the eleven- and twelve-year-old league. I got hit by pitches so many times—it might have been the way I stood in the batter's box—that I lost count.

One game, my first-place team, the Red Sox, was facing the second-place team, the Mets. The Mets were not very good but had a thirteen-year-old who appeared to be six feet tall, 150 pounds. To the rest of us, he looked like a grown man with facial hair. He'd turned thirteen after May 1, the cutoff, so he was eligible to play against us. And let me tell you: This. Kid. Was. Unstoppable.

He would hit two home runs a game. Nobody knew how to pitch against him; he always found his way on base. Due to his strength and manly stature, the Mets put him on the mound as often as they could. When he pitched, the ball crossed home plate in a blur. Although he threw the ball as fast as Pedro Martinez, he had the control of a two-year-old. He was a wild card who threw heat.

When I discovered he was pitching against us that game, I knew I had to figure out how not to get killed by a kid with a lethal weapon for an arm.

I was up to bat. First, I prayed to get walked. Second, I got into the batter's box and waited for a strike. I stood at the far corner of the box, nowhere near the plate. His first three pitches were thrown at about sixty-eight miles per hour, and totally wild. They were outside the strike zone, so far over the catcher's head that the umpire had to provide a new ball after each pitch. The count was three balls and no strikes before the phenom wild-man got smart. He took some gas off the ball and threw two meatballs down the plate for a strike. Suddenly, a full count.

UH OH. Now I have to swing.

I stepped into the box, moved closer to the plate, and waited for the next pitch. The next ball he threw was seventy miles per hour and headed straight toward the left side of my body. I went into survival mode. I used my left hand to smack the ball away from hitting me. I think my hand still has that bruise! I wanted to cry, it hurt so badly. But I didn't. I took first base and repeated to myself Tom Hanks' memorable line: *"There's no crying in baseball!"*

Running down to first base from the batter's box after that at-bat, I noticed I was having difficulty staying on the base path. I'd noticed it repeatedly throughout the season.

Growing up, I'd made a challenge for myself to run directly along the white-chalked path. After I'd run to first, I would look back to see the many footprints I'd made. Now, I would see just two or three imprints at most.

This tormented me. It was another reason sports were no longer as fun as they had been just a year ago. That's why I quit football. Sean did too, though mainly because the practices in August were unbearably hot.

Was I getting worse?

Was everybody else just getting better?

Why was my experience changing so quickly?

I made it through the baseball season with a few more scars. Once the season ended, I decided to stop playing organized baseball. But I didn't want to give up sports completely. Maybe lacrosse might be fun?

I liked being active, but I wanted to try something else, something different. I couldn't wait to begin. Doing different things excites me, because I can learn at my own pace and make them my own. Now, I know I was cocky when I claimed to be so great at other sports, but I can make no such claims about lacrosse. I was athletic enough to keep up, but my hand-eye coordination was seemingly getting worse. I could hit baseballs and shoot hoops, but it seemed to be much harder for me to throw and catch a lacrosse ball.

My coach decided I would play defense, and he loved me because I worked hard and tried to be coachable. I played defense with an edge and was never prone to intimidation. That means I fouled my opponents a lot. Lacrosse is a challenging sport, and the opposing players gave it their all. I felt like such a badass after seeing a yellow flag floating in the air. I would rather foul than have some dude get past me. But I didn't feel so great about being known as the rookie hothead on the field. To learn the game and improve, I watched my older brother, Ryan, and his high school team attentively. I saw how high school players played defense—and what the defenders could get away with—and I incorporated their strategies into my game.

I got better throughout the season. My skills could not help me against bigger players; only a tough mindset would assist me there. I was 120 pounds soaking wet, standing at five feet three inches, and in one game, I covered a kid one-on-one who was about six-one, 190. Remember, we were all thirteen! There was no way I could take him. The laws of the universe were at work. I remembered watching Kobe Bryant talk about mental toughness, so I decided that mind games would be my strategy. Hey, I might have been physically weaker, but my will to succeed was stronger.

I closely guarded this goon for the entire game. I did whatever I had to do to keep him preoccupied. I defended him closely, made sure he did not catch any passes, and I may have gotten away with a few hand checks.

When I was on the field, I just thought about how it's a dog-eat-dog world. I didn't care that I was going against the biggest dog out there. In this game, I looked like a yappy Yorkshire terrier, barking at the Doberman, unaware there was a 100 percent chance the Doberman would eventually bite my head off. I kept throwing jabs at him with my stick.

After the thirtieth poke, the Doberman came at me, gloves off. My instinct was to fight back. I did my best, but he tossed me like a ragdoll while I unsuccessfully swung at him. Luckily, my goalie was almost as big as my rival was. He ran over to defend me, but the referee intervened before it got out of hand. The ref snapped the two of us apart, and our coaches hurried to grab us by the scruffs to escort us back to our sidelines. Later, the ref admitted to my coach, "I couldn't watch that young kid get hurt."

I was a one-and-done lacrosse player.

I was competitive with a desire to fight for myself. I never wanted to seem weak. I feared not being able to live up to my potential as an athlete. But sports were becoming harder. I wasn't playing as much, and my attitude was souring. Internally, I was freaking out. I thought I was losing my identity and that my family and friends would not treat me the same anymore. How can you be in a sports family and not play sports? I cared so much about what others thought of me that I never cared about what I thought of myself. If I got a congratulatory pat on the back from a coach or teammate, or a cheer from a parent in the fan section, I was satisfied. It fed me.

After that lacrosse season, due to my smaller size and under-performance, I asked my parents if I could begin exercising at our local YMCA. Instead, they signed me up to meet with a personal trainer two times a week. I was thirteen, and the thought of working out and beefing up excited me. Susan, my trainer, had me using every machine the gym owned to help me build muscle. I began to curl dumbbells, bench press, test my strength on the leg press, and do abductor work to improve my lateral movement. Susan even had me drinking protein shakes, which made me feel tough. I would tell her some of the challenges I faced when playing sports. We worked on things that felt hard, like catching a basketball pass or outjumping an opponent. We practiced catching and throwing a ten-pound medicine ball. This was an excellent exercise for me at the time. To improve my ability to box out other players on a basketball court, we did extra pullups and pushups to increase my strength.

After a basketball game a few months later, a family friend pulled me aside and gave me a congratulatory hug. He said before he let go, "I can see the work you're putting in in the weight room, and your game shows it. Keep up the great work." I was smiling ear to ear. My exercise regimen was paying off. I was excited to see my training translate into results the next sports season. My hard work when nobody was watching was now being noticed.

CHAPTER 4

That's So Foul

As Sean and I entered sixth grade, we were lucky to go to school with our best friends, Joey G., Rocco, and Petey. We all played basketball together and couldn't get enough of the game. All five of us played for both our school team and our city travel team. Joey G. was a speedy and shifty guard—and a hothead like me. Rocco was a tall, athletic forward, a natural player. Petey was a beast, an unstoppable center. Whether it was boxing out an opponent or setting a screen, Petey won the battle every time, no question.

The Leominster travel team, which consisted of some of the best players in our city, practiced on Mondays and Wednesdays and played games on Sundays. Our school team, St. Anna's, was part of the Catholic Youth Organization (CYO) league. This team consisted of players from our school, practiced on Tuesdays and Thursdays, and played games on Saturdays. Between our travel team and school team, we had basketball every single day except Friday nights. On those nights, we all went to Petey's house and played basketball in his backyard.

Petey's backyard had a large pool, a pool house, an outdoor shower, and a half-sized basketball court. The court had rubber flooring and a stadium light so we could play at night and through the rain or snow. During one of the many snowstorms in Massachusetts, a few of our other buddies joined us for count-less games to twenty-one. While playing basketball in our snow gear, we checked each other into the snow to prevent people from scoring. Since we were all wearing layers and the snow was eight inches high, nobody got hurt. And nobody called fouls.

My dad coached our school team, and he was always supportive of us heading to Petey's to play more basketball. It was a win-win. I needed the practice because I was now physically smaller than the others. It seemed like many of my teammates were beginning to hit their growth spurts, but not me. So, I was the sixth man on the school roster, which means I did not start anymore, but I was first off the bench and always saw court time.

By seventh grade, I'd gotten a lot better by practicing and continuing to work out with Susan at the gym. Strength training really gave me an edge. Eventually, I was playing and contributing more. My hard work was paying off—but the success was short-lived.

After the fifth game, weird things started happening with my body. Not the odd stuff that every pubescent boy feels, like developing gross pimples or hearing my voice suddenly drop a few octaves and sound like a backfiring car muffler. No, this was different. This feeling was more like my legs were not moving as fast as everyone else's or that my muscles fatigued more quickly than others' despite my weight routine.

Why do I trip when running full speed?

Why can't I dribble a basketball down the court?

Why is my twin brother already six inches taller than me and thirty pounds heavier?

Did the rim get smaller, or did the court get longer?

I'd run laps around these chumps in my younger years. Suddenly, I had to focus just to stay balanced.

I figured it was because my growth spurt was behind schedule. Although that didn't seem like the only reason, I went with it.

One of the worst feelings was knowing I was not as physically strong as the other boys. One game, we were up against a team full of all-stars. Their top ten players were five-eight or taller, already went to the weight room, and were fast as hell. Four of them even dunked in warmups during the routine layup lines. Fortunately for me, the opposing team had one kid who was small and not very good. *Probably the coach's son.* We played man-to-man instead of the typical elementary-school zone defense, so every time that kid subbed in, my dad would sub me in to guard him.

I was excited I could finally play, and I didn't care if it was to defend a helpless, smaller kid. So there I was, guarding the runt of the opposing team, and I *still* couldn't keep up. When teammates passed me the ball at half-court to set up the offense, I couldn't catch the ball. I fumbled it out of bounds, tripped over my own feet, and spilled onto the floor. No one was guarding me, but I fell anyway. I was my own worst enemy. I was subbed out, and I shooed away my teammates' pats because the more they did that, the more humiliated I felt.

After that, my game changed. Even during timeouts of games before ours, when kids would go on the open court to shoot during that minute, I never could outrebound anyone, and I was not quick enough to track down the ball. Truthfully, I just went on the court to fit in and not be the only kid sitting alone on the bleachers, knowing I wouldn't touch a ball and counting down the seconds until the timeout ended.

As the basketball season progressed, our team was doing well. We became more competitive with each win. Sean had been playing like a high school player already, and his stats began to stack up. For me, shooting, catching, and passing the ball became harder, even sloppy. It was like a sick joke. I would get the ball, but then I couldn't dribble. Referees called me for traveling all the time. I became more frustrated with every game. I would wait for my dad's coaching instincts to turn on and correct me for my turnover the way he would with others. But when it came to me, he let it go. *Weird.* Instead, he would substitute me out and give me a high-five on my way to the bench.

We have all seen parents coach their kids. Sometimes the parent favors the kid. More often, the parent is harder on their kid than on the other players. For example, my buddy's dad coached him in basketball. During an exhibition game that didn't mean anything, my friend made a few too many turnovers and was not playing well. He was frustrated to the point that he was screaming at the ref, which got him a technical foul for mouthing off. In the middle of the game, his father/coach called a timeout, looked at his assistant coach, and said, "You're in charge." He then grabbed my friend—his son—from the court and walked him to the car mid-game. I never asked my friend what happened after that. I don't think I want to know.

Nothing remotely close to that ever happened to me. My dad stopped getting mad at me when I made a mistake but would be hard on Sean when he rarely screwed up. Mistake after mistake, my father remained calm with me. Instead, I started playing less and less. I went from playing around twenty minutes per game to around five by the end of the season.

At the same time, Sean continued to excel. He was unstoppable on the court. After games, he would actively deflect the glowing attention to spare my feelings. When my sister's attractive new college roommates came to watch us once, I barely played, while

Sean stole the show. I wanted my basketball skills to impress my sister's friends.

Nope.

More important, Sean hated seeing me upset. After games, we would quickly leave the gym even after blowout wins when he scored twenty points. He deserved every accolade, but he selflessly began protecting my pride.

No matter how much I changed my skills or practiced shots to adapt to challenges, my game continued to decline as the championship game approached. *Maybe I should sleep more, because I know you grow in your sleep.* I was still waiting for that growth spurt. Any day now. *Or I should just go back to chess.* That's a sport, right?

CHAPTER 5

FA Night

After a long, hard-fought regular season, the championship game finally arrived. The St. Anna Tigers were undefeated, and we were up against the second-place Catholic Cathedral Bears, who were 16-1 (their only loss was to us). We were confident we could beat them again, given the strength of our team and our overall chemistry. We were playing like a well-oiled machine.

On that cold winter day, my dad, Sean, and I headed to the gym for the championship game. Ryan, who was away at college, called to wish us good luck. We got to the gym an hour before tipoff. I felt like a pro athlete wearing my dark-grey hoodie and baggy sweatpants over my uniform and snow boots. My game sneakers, Nike headband, Kobe Bryant sleeve, and a basketball filled my gym bag. I had on my headphones to listen to Lil Wayne's *Tha Carter III* to pump me up. I felt like The Man when we arrived at the gym. Our team was dialed in and didn't speak to anyone. We remained in the zone.

Tipoff came. We wanted so badly to win. So did the Bears. The game was competitive from the jump, and the score went back and forth. And I stayed on the bench. I had not seen a second of playing time. As the first half ended, I wanted to question why my dad hadn't put me in, but I managed to keep quiet. Sean had played well, yet I was frustrated. I figured since the game was close, I wouldn't play a lot, but I knew my dad would put me in at some point. He knew how much I wanted to play.

The second half started as intensely as the first, with both teams playing with purpose. The Bears took the lead, and with seventeen minutes remaining, we were down by one. I sat on the edge of the bench, just waiting for the signal to get on the court. With twelve minutes left, we regained the lead and were up by three. My blood started to boil.

Maybe I won't play? Wait, that can't happen! That won't happen!

With seven minutes left, we were up by five. I was still on the bench, keeping my seat warm. Then the two-minute warning buzzer rang. Sean and the others had taken control, and we were up by nine. We were going to win the championship. With so much breathing room, my dad finally walked back to where I sat, turned to me, and asked, "Joey, you want in?" I took a look at the other team's bench players checking into the game and was ashamed. Since I did not want to be associated with "lesser" players, I declined. I was hurt that my dad would even put me in this position.

What did I do wrong? What was the point?

We won by eight points. Or, I should say *my teammates* won by eight points. All of my best friends won that game without me. For the first time in my athletic career, I went an entire game without playing. I had gone from star athlete to benchwarmer in just two years, all while my fraternal twin brother kept climbing to become MVP of the game. My head was spinning as my teammates shook the other team's hands.

My confusion fueled my anger, and my anger led to deep sadness—sadness that my natural athletic ability had been lost, and to what, I had no idea. I used to kick ass framing the ball behind home plate, sneakily fooling the umps to get a called strike.

I could play stellar defense, going after guys double and triple my size in football and lacrosse. Now, when my brain told my arm to dribble the ball, nothing happened. My fancy footwork had been replaced by clumsiness and frequent tripping. My reflexes were in slow motion.

While the team cheered and danced around in the locker room, I began changing back into my winter clothes. I was upset that my dad had benched me and did not even offer an explanation. I could not handle seeing parents praise my teammates. I needed to leave the gym as fast as I could. I didn't want any obligatory congratulations hugs. I found my mom and she drove me home.

During the twenty-minute ride, I ranted to my mom about not being as good as everyone else anymore. She stayed patient and let me vent. Then, I did what I hated doing most: I cried—no, I *wailed* like a baby who'd lost his favorite wubba. My mom tried to calm me down, but I couldn't stop. I just needed to get home.

Immediately as the car stopped in our garage, I ran upstairs to my room and continued to cry for what seemed like hours, alone. I tried to cry silently when Sean and my dad got home, but they heard me anyway. I hated myself even more for crying then.

It got very late, but I was nowhere close to sleep. Apparently, neither was my father, who called me into our playroom and sat me down on the couch. He shut off the TV and put his right arm around my shoulders. He was having trouble looking me in the eye. I was ready to brush off his apology for not playing me while ignoring him as he told me how much he loved me and blah blah blah. But he didn't say he was sorry. Instead, he said: "Joey, I need to tell you something I should have told you a while ago. You have Friedreich's ataxia."

And just like that, my whole world came crashing down. I knew it was real, and I did not even question the horrific news. I had the same disease Kaela was battling. In a matter of minutes, I saw my entire life. I'd learned firsthand what was to come from watching Kaela struggle. I'd seen how this disease forced Kaela to stop dancing and playing sports. She started having trouble walking and needed someone to help her to do pretty much everything. All because of FA! She had to stop doing things she loved because her body wouldn't allow her to do them anymore. This was my future now.

At thirteen, I no longer felt invincible or that some good, old-fashioned hard work would solve my problems.

I bolted back to bed sobbing while my parents, Sean, and Kaela followed me in. They all cried with me, trying to assure me that life would be okay. But I was too scared to believe them. I didn't know what to think. The unknown was my new worst enemy. I cried myself to sleep, just so afraid. That day, that night, that moment, and those bone-chilling words have shaped my entire life. FA was a curveball, and in my mind, that meant it was lights out—game over.

When you're growing up, you might desire to be a famous movie star, walking down red carpets with paparazzi everywhere, or the next big musician with eight platinum records. You're living in a big mansion by the ocean somewhere on an exotic island with your beautiful spouse and three kids, whom you teach how to ride a bike, walk, and talk, and preach to about how great chocolate chip pancakes are. Once they grow up, they'll have kids of their own, making you a grandparent who will spoil them with love. Suddenly, I didn't know what to desire or what was realistic for me to anticipate.

That night, when I finally fell asleep, I dreamt of playing a basketball game in front of a sold-out arena. My team was making our way to the court. As we were running out of the locker room to be greeted by the crowd, everyone disappeared. I saw a wheel-chair at the entrance. Suddenly, my legs stopped working, and everything went dark. Except the wheelchair.

CHAPTER 6

Now What?

From that day forward, I thought a lot about fate. Have you ever wondered what it would be like to know your future? To have a clear vision of what your life would be like when you got older? Life would be so much easier if I could see the future like Bran Stark from *Game of Thrones*. I would see my future in detail, including high school, college, my first job, and beyond. Would I be the class president, prom king, or date the most popular girl in school? Would I put my education on hold to go backpacking through Europe to figure out my life's purpose? If Bran had appeared in my bedroom before I'd found out I had FA, I would have definitely freaked out and probably peed my pants. Then, after putting on new pants, I would have asked Bran to show me my fate and the incredible journey I could expect.

Today, Bran was not needed. My fate had been revealed. After the dust settled, I started to think more deeply about my new identity. Usually, when a truth is told, some white lies are also uncovered. These white lies helped keep the secret under wraps. They weren't malicious. They were simply to protect me, to maintain my innocence. Now I started to notice them.

FA was the reason behind my recent athletic struggles, spitting while speaking, balance and coordination issues, fatigue, and muscle soreness. And in learning this truth, I also discovered some of the lies: My parents and older siblings had known about my diagnosis since I was nine years old. They just didn't want to ruin my early life by telling me until I *had* to know. They did their best to make sure I had a typical experience until it was no longer possible.

I was frustrated. How could I be so dumb? So blind? How could I not have put this all together? I didn't even consider that something big was wrong. Every time I felt outmatched in sports, I would mentally shift my attention to work ethic and working out. I'd shut down negative thoughts and push onward. In hindsight, I should have been able to read between the lines. My sister had the disease. I would go to doctor appointments with her every four to six months, thinking my visits were routine checkups to "see why my growth spurt was delayed." I should have been suspicious that these appointments were with neurologists at Massachusetts General Hospital, not with our primary care doctor a few miles away.

I do have to admit, one cool part about having so many doctor appointments included skipping so much school. Sometimes my parents would tell me I had the day off or they were going to sign me out early. I felt like a rock star when my whole classroom would hear over the PA, "Please send Joseph Mullaney down to the office. He's leaving for the day." I *watched the clock* in anticipation of that announcement, waiting to grab my already packed bookbag and bolt for the door.

See ya later, everyone. Enjoy learning cursive and long division!

I did think it was strange that Sean never got called. But I shrugged it off and focused on how quickly I could get in my parents' car so we could go to the McDonald's drive-through before hitting the highway. And we got to take trips into downtown Boston, which felt magical to me, even on days I would get poked and prodded with needles. My family was lucky to have lived only an hour from Boston, home to some of the world's best hospitals, including MGH, Brigham and Women's, Tufts, and Boston Children's. Boston is swarming with fantastic pediatric specialists, neurologists, and rare disease doctors.

As for why I needed to go to the doctor so frequently, "The doctor could help you with your strength and balance," my parents said. "After the appointments, we'll take you and Kaela to eat wherever you both want." I welcomed the thought of a doctor being able to help me with my basketball skills. The delicious food was just a bonus.

Man, I loved traveling through the streets of Boston and seeing Fenway Pahhkk, the Charles River, the Prudential Center Building, the FleetCenter (before it was TD Garden). It felt like a world away from my classroom back in the 'burbs. There were thousands of people walking around like they were an hour late for their graduation. Cars, trucks, and taxis were everywhere, filling the air with a cacophony of honking sounds. I thought crossing the street was illegal during a red light, but everyone still did it—even cops! *This is where the action is. I'll live here one day,* I vowed.

FA diminished the wonder of Boston. I thought to myself, *How could you live in a big city when you can't even walk? How can you use a public bathroom if you can't stand up and pee? How can you live anywhere if you might not be able to eat alone?*

The day after FA Night, Sean and I were back in school. Before school started, Sean and I played four square on the playground with our other classmates who had gotten to school early that day. Sean and I acted like nothing had happened, pretending like our lives hadn't massively changed just twelve hours ago.

No matter my game face, though, I could not stop thinking about it. As I stood there in my square, bouncing the ball before serving it, I felt divided from my friends by more than the boxes we were defending. Fortunately, my friends didn't pick up on the fact that I felt as if I'd just seen a ghost.

And that ghost kept showing me my future of being buried in the ground, while my family and friends surrounded my casket because FA had killed me.

The ball came to me, and I tried to hit it back. I hit the ball the wrong way, and it jammed my thumb and bruised my wrist. Based on my reaction, you would have thought a sniper on the roof had shot me. To say I was jumpy is an understatement. I was trying to process everything while also playing it cool. On the surface, I looked okay. Deep down, I was hurting. This thumb bruise had cracked open my pent-up emotions.

This is NOT right! I am NOT okay! What in the hell? I'm only thirteen years old! I still haven't even hit puberty!

I was lost and afraid. But still, I hopped back in line and quietly waited my turn.

At times, I felt unaware about what I still could do, and that feeling of confusion led to frustration. I'd barely survived the summer of the cyst. I started thinking back to that summer and wondering if I'd actually needed that wheelchair or if the doctors had thought it would be an excellent way for me to familiarize myself with it for the future. I mistrusted everything and everyone, questioned things I never had before.

It was a hard disillusionment for a thirteen-year-old. I had questions. And I wanted answers. One month after finding out, I sat down with my parents.

"So, why did I go to those doctor appointments in Boston?" I asked Mom and Dad.

"The doctors were trying to monitor your progression of FA," they said truthfully.

"Did Ryan and Kaela know?"

No answer.

"Why was Sean also crying on FA Night? Did he know too?"

No answer.

"How could you keep this from me? Why didn't you all tell me?"

They were not sure how to answer. They were visibly emotional.

I did not mean for that last question to make my parents cry, but it did. I now understand that they wanted to preserve my innocence as long as possible. I now know how hard it was for both my parents. They did their best. Today it makes more sense. But back then, I was unsatisfied. I just wanted answers to these pressing questions.

I am of two minds here. Usually, when you have information about a loved one that will significantly impact their lives, you should tell them. No hesitation. But how would you describe to your son that he has a disease that will paralyze his body slowly and progressively until he dies? There is no rule book to follow, so my family did what they thought was right.

That night, I kept firing questions at my parents.

"Is this why you had me working out? Not to help me grow, but to keep my muscles engaged?"

"Yes," my parents answered. "Doctors recommended that it would help slow down muscle atrophy."

"How fast is the disease spreading? What does a progressive illness even mean? How long before I'm in a wheelchair?"

My parents were even more emotional now, and they struggled to answer me.

"Tell me!" I yelled.

But their silence and sad faces were the only answers I needed.

CHAPTER 7

Well, This Sucks

Denial is the first step. When someone receives life-changing news, it cuts to the core. The typical immediate reactions are to reject or dismiss the idea entirely and push the situation far away. Even with all the remaining questions I had, I was not comfortable, at the age of thirteen, talking with anyone. So, nobody—besides Google, which I quickly stopped using—could tell me about how FA worked and why it happens. After a couple of searches, I saw that FA will eventually make my heart stop. From then on, I did not want to learn anything else about FA. I did not care how it worked or why I had it. Did. Not. Care.

I told myself, "Be an athlete and deal with it on your own; face problems as they come." I was not open to learning anything about FA, except what I observed from watching my sister.

I did not care to understand the disease's symptoms and difficulties, like a weakening heart, potential for diabetes, and speech impediments. I figured that what I didn't know couldn't hurt me. If I didn't understand what was coming, somehow I would be better off. Ignorance is bliss, right?

Even though I knew I had FA, I was determined to hide it. I did not want to tell a living soul, not even my best friends, about my condition. Keeping that massive secret changed me. It tainted me. And it started to show.

Now that I knew my fate, I became even more jealous of Sean. I wanted to be the guy who scored thirty points a game. I wanted to dribble past three defenders and make an and-one layup, too.

I wanted the accolades from parents and coaches and super-fans, too. *I* wanted to play high school sports, too. That was supposed to be how it went for Sean and me.

Now what?

What of "The Mullaney Twins"?

What about our sports family?

I was afraid I would forever be known as the "sick twin." The unlucky kid. The kid who played chess.

I chose not to tell my friends about FA for a few reasons. First, I did not want them to pity me. Second, and more important, I did not have the heart to tell them. I did not know the proper way to explain it. My entire family, and mostly Sean, agreed with my position. He had my back through all of this. Sean knew I did not want to tell our friends, which I realize now put him in a position to lie or withhold the truth.

I was shy and secretive about my condition, but certain adults in my life had to know. I did not think it would be so soon after FA Night, but a few days later, as I walked to my homeroom during lunch period, I saw my parents walk out of the principal's office along with my homeroom teacher. They were walking way too close to each other and said their goodbyes more personally than what seemed typical. The personal-space boundary seemed to be crossed by a shoulder grab, a tilted head, or a double-fisted handshake, and I knew exactly why. They were now intimately involved with my business.

My teacher was a stern lady who rarely smiled and demanded good behavior at all times. She and I never saw eye to eye—let's just put it that way.

Now, though, every time I saw her, she looked at me like I was a puppy who needed love. She gave me the kind of look you give a guy who drops his coffee as he leaves Dunkin', or a stressed-out mom carrying one child on her hip while the other three nag her for candy in the grocery store—you just thank goodness you're not that person. You feel for them, but your look says, "That sucks for you." Yay for me! Soon all the teachers would know it sucks to be Joey.

The next day, before we went to lunch, my teacher called my best friend, Petey, and me to deliver a package to the principal's office with instructions to head straight to lunch before the rest of our classmates went. Our homeroom was on the second floor of the building, and the cafeteria was in the basement.

Petey thought it was strange that our teacher asked us to do this almost twenty minutes before lunch began, but I knew exactly why. She didn't want me walking down two flights of stairs with the rest of my classmates who could knock me over, so she made up some crazy story to try to help me. I didn't want Petey or any of my other classmates to know what was really going on, so I had to act confused. Honestly, I could have received an Oscar for my performance. Petey had no clue why we were getting out of class early. And we were both psyched because we would not have to wait in line in the cafeteria.

For the rest of the year, my teacher helped me. Going down a flight of stairs at recess or lunchtime with 300 other students was becoming impossible for me. It was easy for me to get hit and lose my balance. Every day, my teacher would use the envelope delivery as a diversion to give me a head start. Though I hated this, I just went with it. I didn't want to get hurt. But I knew it wouldn't be long before the class got tired of me being picked all the time to run errands and leave the room early, so I strategized.

I acted weird or protested when I was excused. Once, I told the teacher I felt sick before she asked Petey and me to deliver some-thing. Even though I was fine, she allowed Petey to walk with me to the nurse's office twenty minutes before lunch. The nurse immediately advised me to eat something to help me feel better.

Strategy.

My teacher and I (and the slew of other teachers in the school) were in a ruse together: the save-face-for-Joey ruse. I'd wanted to avoid that kind of treatment initially, but I knew it was necessary. My attitude still sucked, and I planned on just copping out of life.

CHAPTER 8

Pivot Foot

In the Christopher Reeve *Superman* movie, Clark Kent finds out the reasons why he was awkward at school. He learns why he can throw a football the length of five football fields, outrun a freight train, and hear a high-pitched whistle from miles away. He's an alien!

I, too, felt like an alien—but a fat, ugly, green alien with three heads and giant antennae for ears. I could only wish my reasons for not fitting in were as cool as Clark's. Clark chose not to accept the facts about his life right away, whereas I really had no choice. But Clark and I did have one thing in common: We each built our own fortress of solitude. Mine, of course, wasn't made of sparkling crystals. It was just a place in my mind where I battled confusion and denial.

It was a hot summer day before I entered eighth grade when I tracked down my dad in the backyard to announce my decision to quit basketball. My father was not having any of my attempts at solitude. "You can't quit. Not yet," he said to me.

I just wanted to begin my new life, in eighth grade, by playing chess and video games. I thought it would be more comfortable for me to let sports go on my terms, before FA took more of its toll.

Dad pushed his lawnmower into our garage, and with sweat trickling down his face, he told me he understood.

"Don't let FA stop you, but I see your perspective," he said.

Just when I thought he got it, he followed up with, "But it

would be a shame, Joe, to go into eighth grade and not play on your team for your last year of grade school. End of an era, you know?"

I knew I wouldn't be known as a jock in high school. I would be starting over in a new school, creating a new identity soon enough, but this time on much different footing.

Maybe I was rushing it. Perhaps I should stay on the team. Dad said if I didn't, I'd have regrets.

To be honest, quitting just seemed a lot easier than playing with a disability. But I did want to enjoy the time spent with Joey G., Petey, Rocco, Sean, and the rest of my teammates. Sports were as social for me as they were athletic. Although watching games from the bench would be miserable, postgame celebrations would be grand. I loved going to Applebee's or Pizza Hut with my teammates. If I quit, I would lose all of that.

"Let me help you, Joe," Dad said, resting his hand on my shoulder. "I've got some ideas."

Dad knew puberty would eventually rear its ugly head. When it did, there would be the right mix of hormones to strengthen my weak muscles. I desperately needed some of those hormones, fast! I could not keep going up for a layup in practice and having a defender like Petey send me crashing to the floor. I needed a program to help me with FA specifically. Claim those muscles before FA claimed them!

We began exercising to prepare for the next basketball season. I had seen my brother Ryan work out during the summertime. He would use all the weights, but I never really understood what he was doing. All I knew was he was gearing up for another year of sports. Ryan would curl dumbbells, deadlift some hexagonal bar-thingy, and in between sets, he would drop down and do pushups or situps. If we were down in the cellar simultaneously, we would work out together. He showed me the basics like pushups, squats, and jump rope, and he was thrilled every time I wanted to work out with him. Ryan, along with my dad, would go into coach mode and try to teach me things.

Dad bought a leg-press machine for the basement and then introduced the idea of bulking up my arms so I could use them to help me one day transfer my body from a wheelchair to a bed, chair, couch, etc.

Fortunately, my dad was a general contractor. He and his crew installed grab bars throughout my home for Kaela and me to place our hands on while we walked. That helped. Weightlifting would build my arms so I could grab on and pick myself up. Then I graduated to curling heavy dumbbells for my biceps and doing body-weight dips to activate and strengthen my triceps. I even began using a boxing speedbag we put in the "gym-basement." This was great for motor skills and hand-eye coordination, both of which were threatened by FA. After exhausting myself doing all of this, I would shoot hoops in the backyard, so I could be as athletic as possible with the limitations I had.

When basketball season arrived a few months later, my attitude was a little better, and I was ready to play. Before the first game, my dad faithfully took me to the basketball court on our driveway. He taught me how to play basketball with a strategy that worked with my physical condition. That's right—work *with* it, not against it. Preserve what you still possess. I had broad shoulders, so we developed ways to use them to help box out an opponent. Oddly, my idea of not being in control of a progressive disease went away for a little bit, especially when I was working out and training. At least I could control how hard I tried and how much I learned. I always had control over pivoting, physically and mentally, to what I wanted to do next.

For example, since my dad knew that dribbling a basketball wasn't an option for me anymore, he told me how to catch the ball properly. That way, I could either shoot or pivot to pass without making any unnecessary movements. He taught me that when you catch a basketball, you don't have to shoot or dribble immediately. You could plant one foot—your pivot foot—and still move the other. Pivoting helped me stay balanced and dangerous with the ball in my hands.

I could still add some value on the court. I could catch, shoot, or pass. I also practiced shooting the ball as soon as I grabbed it to avoid balance issues and throw the defense off guard.

Even with dad's help, I wasn't gaining as much ground as I wanted. FA was worsening my hand-eye coordination. Nevertheless, we kept working. As hard as it was to admit that I had limitations, acknowledging them helped me get mentally stronger. Even though my body was up against a formidable opponent, I was mentally up for the fight. Like when Rocky faced that crazy Russian boxer who had already killed a guy in the ring. Now, I was the American boxer training in Siberia. I was Clark Kent examining Jor-El's crystals. The more I allowed myself to see new ways of doing things, the less I feared my future with FA.

My victory-lap season started, and I continued to learn how to weight train to strengthen my body. The practicing and pivots were working, and I also figured out that I could minimize the incidences of losing balance and falling on my face if I learned to take shots without moving.

After adjusting my game to my body, my mindset about being a teammate shifted. Instead of trying to be like Kobe Bryant, which

I had always dreamed of, I focused on having fun and playing like Brian "Scal" Scalabrine. I became a great "locker room guy."

Scal was one of the best bench players ever to play in the NBA. He was most definitely a locker room guy, and I loved watching him play for the Celtics. He brought humor and enjoyment to his teammates and fans through his antics on and off the court. He certainly was not the best player on the 2007-08 Boston Celtics championship team, but during the few minutes he would play, Scal heaved up three-point shots. No matter the result, his bold attempts got teammates roaring from the bench and fans cheering like crazy in the stands. Scal did not care about how little he played. He always made the most of his time on the court.

With my last basketball season under way, I was the sixth-man-turned-benchwarmer. I was also the morale booster for my teammates. I mentally pivoted and accepted my new role on the team. I followed Scal and became a hardworking and fun teammate. Even if I couldn't score thirty points a game or ferociously block a defender, I could pretend to dunk a basketball in practice by fake-jumping six and a half feet to get my teammates to laugh and relax. I mastered the art of the celebration on the bench by shooting imaginary arrows around the gym, pretending to be Katniss Everdeen from *The Hunger Games*. The idea of not being on a team at all was more upsetting than coming off the bench.

At the beginning of my eighth-grade season for our city travel team, we played in the biggest basketball showcase for our age group. Led by Sean, our team was very talented, and we were facing the best competition in the state of Massachusetts. Even Danny Ainge, the Celtics' general manager, was there watching his son play. I knew I was not going to see any playing time. I also knew my teammates wanted badly to win, so I took a break from my usual clowning around and put on a serious face for them. As a benchwarmer, the showcase wasn't as exciting to me as it was to my teammates. My mom even said I could play my PSP between games!

But in our last game, we were ahead by twenty-seven points.

"You're in," the coach said to me, patting me on the back. I saw on the scoreboard that there was still time left, so I was confused. I had not prepared for playing time; I was just lasered in on playing PSP again when the game ended. But when I got off the bench and went to check in, I channeled my inner Scal.

My new game plan replaced my normal anxiety about losing balance or falling: *Get the ball far away from the hoop, hold it with strength, and don't mess up.* I had practiced this game plan as I figured out how to adapt my skill set to my current abilities. The idea was that if I didn't dribble or move, I wouldn't turn the ball over or get called for traveling.

PLOT TWIST. Suddenly I had the ball miles behind the three-point line with two seconds left on the shot clock. I did not want to shoot, but my teammates were yelling at me, "SHOOT IT!"

So, I launched it. In the shooting process, I lost control of my body, fell back, and hit the floor.

"Kobe!"

Nailed it. The crowd and my teammates went berserk. It was my first and last three-point shot. The decibel level in the gym made it feel like I'd just hit a shot to win the NBA Finals.

Honestly, I never saw Sean more ecstatic than after my Kobe Bryant moment. He just kept jumping on top of me with excitement, knocking me over and catching me before I fell. It almost seemed as if Sean was the one who had made the big shot. (And on numerous occasions, he had!) Sean was so fired up that night.

And he passed his excitement on to my teammates, who got pumped up at the sight of Sean's sweaty, bright-red face.

We all went back into the locker room, and Rocco grabbed his wireless speaker and played "Empire State of Mind" by Jay-Z and Alicia Keys. That song gets the blood pumping, and our team went nuts celebrating. Petey flicked the lights, making it feel like we were in a V.I.P. room in a Las Vegas club. Rocco blasted the volume, and we began our version of dancing—basically jumping and pushing each other—right there in the locker room. I didn't fall once the whole time because my teammates held me up. It was as if all of them knew about my secret.

After watching me spend numerous games on the bench, suffer through FA Night, and try to manage all the insecurities about my new situation, Sean was just happy I finally got a break. Even though he was the reason we won, he allowed me to take all the glory and attention. At least I would go out on top.

Honestly, I do well in the spotlight. I'm not shy about it, and I feed off the energy of people. It's ironic that the one who deserves the limelight, Sean, doesn't like it much. This was the night we traded places, took on the other's roles—except it lasted beyond the locker room that night and has continued throughout our lives. Seeing that I grew in confidence with each positive response I received—whether it was laughter at one of my jokes, applause for an idea I had, or a simple assist on the basketball court—Sean chose to blend in with the walls. He became the reserved and quiet twin, and since he was so humble anyway, he seemed comfortable in his new role. That is the irony of twins: We're never really the same.

Sean and I were the first set of twins in our family. My parents loved telling us the story of our birth and how we were like a sideshow, with more visitors than usual who wanted to gawk at us. Grammy, my family's matriarch, skipped out of her meetings to be in the hospital waiting room. This was a big deal because at the time, she was an elected official on the city council of her hometown, Fitchburg, Massachusetts. She loved politics and devoted her life to what she believed in. That night she promptly left her city council meeting to attend to family matters. After her daughter gave birth to two boys—Grammy's fifth and sixth grandchildren—she gave everyone big kisses and showered us with attention. Later that night, she drove back to her meeting to catch the end. She walked in late, initially angering her peers. However, when she told everyone why she was late, they all cheered! Her devotion to politics paid off a few years later when she was elected the first female mayor of Fitchburg. Grammy continues to be an inspiring figure to us all.

As fraternal twins, Sean and I look like brothers, but we don't look the same, as identical twins do. Even today, when strangers see us, they can only tell we're somehow related. Sean and I do not have many similarities in behavior, voice, facial expressions, or anything else that would make us seem like carbon copies. But when we were little, people thought we were equally cute. Unfortunately, we were so cute that in first grade, our music teacher asked us to sing a duet at the school concert. We had no choice. Again we were a sideshow. We had no musical talent whatsoever, so we sang terribly while looking adorable.

One of our buddies was convinced that twins could feel each other's pain. He would often sneak up on one of us and pinch us on the arm, then quickly turn his head to the other twin to see his reaction. The experiment never worked, but he always tried, even though we'd pinch him right back—harder.

During our younger years, Sean was a chubby, tall kid with crooked teeth. I was an average-height, skinny kid with freckles and Bucky Beaver teeth. We both had to get braces. We had the same best friends but had different relationships with them. We shared bunk beds in our room. We played on every team together (probably to make it easier for my parents to make one trip). When my parents first allowed us to have cell phones, they were for emergencies only. We got matching green Verizon Migos, which only were capable of having four numbers programmed, one being 911. The other three were our dad, our mom, and our home phone.

Sean hit his growth spurt at the age of twelve. I didn't. By fourteen, Sean had grown to five-eight, while losing all of his baby fat. But I was still a pipsqueak standing about five-two, or five-three with shoes!

That night after my Kobe shot, you would've thought some college dude was patting a fifth-grader on the back. Instead, it was my twin congratulating me. Between the ages of twelve and fifteen, Sean was one of the largest kids on the court and in class.

I began freshman year of high school at only five-three, and I weighed the same as a dozen basketballs. Thankfully, by the winter of sophomore year, I had grown to five-ten, though I was still a skinny kid. Puberty and growth spurts do not make sense. It sucks when you're a pipsqueak playing sports and your twin brother is double your size. I wanted to grow as tall as Sean, so I did whatever I could to catch up. I purposely would go to bed early and sleep in late, believing I would grow in my sleep. I would stretch my legs out as far as possible before I fell asleep and hold them for minutes. But that didn't work. Finally, once I stopped thinking about getting my body to grow, I grew.

Sean and I knew the eighth-grade locker room moment would be one of the last I would have on a team. The games were numbered, and as they came to a close, we were on the losing end of the season. It was not the games I was going to miss so much, though. All of the hard offseason training days when my brothers and I would go through rigorous exercise drills, shooting 100 shots each until we were sweating (and smelling) like pigs before heading inside to eat dinner ... those were behind me now. All of the fun Applebee's trips after games, the car rides with my teammates, and Friday night scrimmages at Petey's were over. My childhood dream of being a professional athlete was just a dream. I knew there would be a day when FA would make me stop playing, but nothing is ever real until it happens.

After our final game, although we all had the same sense that an era was ending—a team was dismantling after we'd played together for years—the other guys did not have the same feeling of finality that I did. They knew they were going to play in high school, but they were sad because we were all splitting up. I knew my playing days were over. The simplest things, like buying a new pair of Jordans, packing my gym bag, or wearing a team jersey to begin a new season, were no longer among the details of my life. I didn't know what my new details would be.

PART II

The Call

CHAPTER 9

High School: A Whole New Ballgame

Part of growing up is the realization that things that were once ordinary are now complicated.

For me, going from eighth grade to high school was definitely more complex than I'd expected. It was a change that hurt, because it meant the disbanding of my friend group. Since sixth grade, we'd all assumed we would go to the same high school together, but we were wrong.

Jon, one of the best hockey players in our city, went to a hockey-focused high school. My cousin Bella was dominant on the lacrosse field, and Petey and Joey G. remained ferocious on the football field and basketball court. Those two, along with Bella, stayed together. Rocco initially went to school with those three and played football, basketball, and baseball, but he eventually transferred to the school where Sean and I ended up, for sports-related reasons.

For me, though, picking a high school had nothing to do with sports. It had everything to do with FA.

Remember those details I mentioned? The ones that made up my life as I knew it and melted away overnight? I had to accept that they were gone. I knew I needed new details to fill my life, but I didn't know if I would ever find any. The only thing I did know is that there is nothing worse than a combination of change and the unknown.

Before giving up on researching FA online, I read as many Facebook posts as I could find written by other people with FA.

I wanted to know how they coped, and they all had the same underlying message: NEVER LET FA DICTATE HOW YOU LIVE YOUR LIFE. As admirable as that message was, it made me think about how I could, realistically, do that. *How could it not control you if every choice you make throughout your life is affected by the future FA has in store for you?*

FA seemed to be driving all my decisions. I had to stop wearing certain shoes because I developed a massive arch in my foot. My hand-eye coordination got so bad, I couldn't tie a tie anymore, which ruled out certain high schools with dress codes.

Already, FA felt like a life-defining "detail"!

Not off to a great start.

Most people go to high school in their towns with their friends, or they pick a sports-focused high school close to where they live. Or, maybe they go wherever their older siblings went. But for me, there were special considerations you don't think of until you have a disease like FA. What really sucked was that these considerations for me also affected Sean. (Though, as usual, he just went with the flow.)

My two older siblings went to the high school near where we grew up. My parents, my mom's three siblings, a few of my older cousins, and my grandparents were also alumni. Ryan and Kaela both enjoyed their high school experiences. Ryan, like Sean, was athletic, excelling in football, basketball, and lacrosse. Kaela played basketball for a year and played field hockey all four years, too. I still have no idea how she physically did it, but she did. Growing up, Sean and I were at the school a lot to watch our cousins', Kaela's, and Ryan's games. We met a lot of people there and just assumed we would go there, too. But FA had different plans.

That building was old—like built-in-the-1920s old—and hadn't changed in many years. It would have been a burden for me, physically. Suddenly, my whole family had to consider me and my future condition and whether the high schools we were thinking about could suit my physical needs. *Were the hallways wide enough for me? Were there too many staircases? How large was the campus?* These were questions I'd never thought about before. Ryan and Kaela's high school had far too many stairs, which pained Kaela during her final years there.

Years later, I discovered my siblings' high school was an older building that didn't have level stairs or an elevator. That blew my mind, but we had to deal with the reality.

Onward and upward. We looked elsewhere. My only demand was that no matter where I went, I did not want people knowing I had FA. We looked at three schools that were "Joey-friendly" (handicap-accessible). We chose Lawrence Academy Preparatory School (LA) in Groton, Massachusetts.

Sean and I shadowed two students for a day, going to some classes with them and seeing how the teachers interacted. Those two students just happened to be star athletes who were beloved on campus. Going with them to their classes, touring their dorm, and eating lunch with them, all while meeting hundreds of new people, made us feel like big men on campus. We loved it!

But a prep school? Us? We grew up eating McDonald's while covered in dirt, and we had rips in our clothes from backyard brawls. Now, I would have to wear fancy clothes with popped collars and eat salmon and lobster. So on day one, when we both wore Nike T-shirts, cargo shorts, and brand-new white sneakers, Sean and I weren't sure if we would fit in.

LA is a coeducational preparatory school with about 400-450 students. Since the school was close to Leominster, Sean and I did not live on campus. About half the kids did, and the other half were day-students, like Sean and me. Some of the guys dressed as if they'd just come back from their summer home in Cape Cod, wearing boat shoes, a Vineyard Vines shirt, and either salmon-colored or light khaki shorts. Girls were wearing sundresses with flip-flops. But a fair number of kids wore regular athletic clothing. LA had a diverse crowd of kids, and our outfits were fine.

About seventy percent of the students were from towns in New England. Twenty percent were athletes from across the United States and Canada who would go on to play a collegiate sport. And ten percent were from other countries like Spain, Germany, South Korea, Russia, or Japan.

LA sits upon a giant hill. At the top, there are academic buildings, a cafeteria, a student lounge, and a few dorms. As you move down the hill, there are a few more dorms. Then down farther is the athletic center. This building consists of locker rooms, a basketball court, a wrestling room, a weight room, a cardio room, the athletic trainers' room, and small offices. At one end of the hill sits the football field and, on the opposite side, the baseball field.

At LA, I could still walk around the large campus and nobody would notice my unsteadiness unless they followed me with a camera like someone from TMZ. Out of all 450 students and faculty, nobody said anything to me about my gait. A person watching me walk may have raised their eyebrow, but I did not focus on that. I walked as if I'd just done two shots of tequila—so, not totally out of it, but slightly buzzed. But FA is only a physical disease, so mentally, I was sharp as a tack.

Each student at LA is part of an advisory group of seven to eight kids from across all grade levels. The group is run by a faculty member. Since Sean was going to try out to play on the varsity basketball team, the coach, Kevin "Coach Kev" Wiercinski, wanted to get to know him and immerse him into the community. I didn't know this before the morning of our first day, but there were many more high-level athletes at LA than I'd realized. And because my twin had the potential to move onto the next level in basketball, LA might have thought I did too.

So they put me in a group led by the assistant football coach, along with four giant Division I-caliber football players and two strong Division I-caliber hockey players. The average size of those six kids was roughly six-two, 200 pounds. Then there I was at five-three, weighing in at 125—a featherweight at best. Although they all were physically intimidating, I wanted to find a way for them to like me.

After the emasculating morning, Sean and I went to different homerooms for the first time. As alone as I felt, I knew that at fourteen years old, it was time to grow up. None of the other kids in the class spoke to one another; we did not even look at one another as we tentatively took our alphabetically assigned seats. At least we were all in the same boat, and knowing that Sean and I had the same lunch period helped make the morning's growing pains bearable.

While walking through the halls, I purposely skimmed the lockers' sides, keeping them close as a safety net, like ropes around a boxing ring. If my drunken walk threw me off balance, at least a wall would be able to spring me upright again before anyone could notice. It seemed like a successful strategy, which I gauged because nobody stared at me or even saw me at all. I had never been so happy to be ignored. However, I sure noticed one thing—and fast. High school girls—especially the upperclassmen—were attractive. Some looked like the models I'd see in magazines.

Each student was required to participate in at least one extra-curricular activity, whether it was a sport, dance, theater, news-paper, debate team, etc. Sean and I did not have a regular fall sport to play, so we tried out for the freshman soccer team. On the first day of tryouts, all thirty of us freshmen had to warm up by running around the entire field. During the run—which I should not have done, but I wanted to fit in—I sprained my ankle. And so I returned to a place I was no stranger to: the bench. Honestly, the injury was a blessing in disguise because it became an excuse in case anyone asked about why I walked the way I did. The doctor made me wear a walking boot for two weeks, and as I got to know new people over the first semester, I was able to milk my twisted ankle. I sat on the bench all soccer season, and even though my foot healed before the end of it, I chose not to play, explaining that I was afraid I'd reinjure my ankle. The only downfall (or uprise?) was not joining my classmates on the annual hiking trip to Mount Monadnock.

But just when I thought I had devised the perfect cover, FA kept finding ways to blow it—for Sean too. Sean and I went to grab lunch one day with a few of our classmates. I was carrying a cup of water, and one of our new friends noticed my hand shaking.

From what I remember, these involuntary tremors first happened while I was in the shower and reached for my shampoo bottle. I shook so badly, I dropped the bottle on the floor. I tried to convince myself that because I'd had a soda that day, the caffeine had given me the jitters (even though it was a caffeine-free soda). These shaky moments occurred about once every two months. If I had an episode in front of people, I would take the comedic route and introduce myself as Kramer from *Seinfeld*. This time, I tried to use twin telepathy to get Sean to grab the cup from me before my grip gave out. But I knew my brother was no mind reader, and I would have to face whatever was coming on my own.

"Better not spill," our new classmate, Alex, said as I passed her at the table full of six other kids. Then she giggled and asked, "Why are you shaking like that?" Alex was my friend, and she wasn't trying to hurt my feelings. Before I could react, and instead of telling her the truth, I took the comedic way out.

"My bad, Alex," I responded, with a fake laugh and an awkward pause between my words. "I drank three cups of coffee today, and I can't stop jittering!"

I don't even drink coffee. Sean just sat there with a sad look, watching me as I lied to hide the truth.

CHAPTER 10

Outside Underneath a Tree at Night in the Fall

Girls, girls, girls. That was what was on my mind throughout my initial days at Lawrence Academy. There might have been no more than six girls in my classroom throughout elementary school and junior high, maximum. And one of those girls was my cousin. Now, there were at least fifteen per class and many more around campus. At LA, I was surrounded by beautiful girls.

Before, I had used my athletic skills to help me flirt. Now, I did not know the first thing about how to act. I used to think girls would be into my athleticism, because who doesn't like an athlete?! But as I stumbled on my feet as though I were always two tequila shots deep, my chances were as low as the lines on the highway.

The summer before high school, I binge-watched *The Office*. Two of the show's primary characters were Jim and Pam. Although they were not a couple at first, everyone knew these two were into each other. They flirted a lot, but it took them a couple of seasons to express how they truly felt. It felt like forever before Jim mustered the courage to confess his love to Pam.

I enjoyed watching Jim because he was quirky and did not look like a typical guy who automatically gets the pretty girl. Pam is beautiful, and if he could win her over, he'd be dating up. I wanted to understand what Jim had going for him that appealed to Pam. Then, I realized it was his personality. Sure, Jim wasn't scoring three-pointers or hitting home runs, but he could make Pam laugh with his quick wit. Jim listened well and was confident in himself. That was what I now needed: a witty personality, charm, compassion, and confidence.

There was a beautiful girl, Maddie, in my homeroom. She was a day-student like me, and she started on the field hockey team. Maddie had long, dirty-blonde hair and an infectious smile. She was shy, but it was time for me to channel my inner Jim to try to win her over with my charm.

During the first few weeks of school, I'd joke with Maddie and try to sit near her in class. Even though I knew the answers to homework questions, I played dumb and asked her for help. When Maddie smiled at me, I would glow with excitement. When I made her laugh even when my jokes were not funny, I knew I'd won her over. We began to walk to classes together, meet up in the student lounge during our mutual free periods, and sit together on the quad after school. Unlike Jim, I didn't have two seasons of episodes to tell Maddie how I felt. The fall dance was upon us, so I had to take my chance.

Like most kids, I hated dances in junior high. They felt like some type of torture device that adults put together to humiliate kids. It was like a science experiment, throwing new kids together with their hormones raging, insecurities blaring, and not knowing how to dance. But high school dances were different. They consisted of loud music in a dark room, chaperones standing outside of the pit of kids, and guys and girls dancing very close to each other. Even the kids who had zero dancing skills would get out there. Dances were not awkward anymore unless you stood there and acted cool, like a wannabe tough guy that nobody likes.

The dance was in late October. By then, Sean and I had made a solid group of friends, including a guy named Mitch. A fellow freshman, Mitch was a very humble, shy kid and hated bragging or being considered pompous by others. But he was a widely known lacrosse player in New England and had been a renowned recruit; he was referred to by the senior LAX players as "Cannon."

When the day of my first high school dance finally came, I walked into school pale as if I had painted myself in Elmer's glue, except for my red-hot cheeks. I was slightly hyperventilating. Sean had to meet with a teacher right away, so I went into the student lounge alone. I found Cannon, and he could tell I was nervous. I mean, he wasn't blind! He looked at me and said, "Let's skip the small talk. I can see your sweat even though it's a windy fall day. There is nothing to stress about, Joey! If you get too tired or anything, just let me know, and I can help. We'll have a fun night, and we'll all have a blast." We heard the bell, so Cannon and I went to class. I was silent.

Wait, what? How did Cannon know I was nervous about getting tired?

Then it hit me like a sucker punch to the gut: SEAN.

I didn't hear a word in any of my classes that morning. If the teacher told us to turn to page fifty in our textbooks, I'd turn to 150. If I dropped a pencil, I didn't notice. I had SEAN on the brain. *This is what twins are for? To betray you? I'm going to kill you, Sean.*

Getting out of class early after I finished my science quiz, which I failed since my mind was elsewhere, I sat silently at the lunch table later that day with the other speedy quiz-takers. I then mapped out my initial plan. When Sean walked in with his classmates, I was going to grab him by the collar, drag him to the bathroom, lock the door, and scream: "How the hell does Cannon know, Sean?!"

In the movies, the snitch's usual response would be, "Know what? I don't know what you're talking about!" But Sean is no actor, and he would know what I meant. I knew he'd told Cannon about FA.

I would yell, "SEAN! Now Cannon is going to pity me and think I'm weak! Cannon is going to tell everyone. You blew the dance for me!"

I was all in my head.

When I saw Sean enter the cafeteria, I channeled my inner Irish-Italian anger and walked right toward him. But instead, I stopped my angry march when I was about three steps from my table. I decided to turn around and walk back.

Sean had done the right thing.

At the time, I didn't think about the fact that Sean was trying to make sure I was okay. Back then, I couldn't see it this way; I thought Sean had hired me a babysitter. But it was for the best. Since our schedules were different, he couldn't be there to help me. But Cannon was with me all day in class, so he could help me carry my heavy books, my backpack, or whatever I needed. Cannon could even sit behind me in almost every class so that when I dropped a pen or a notebook on the floor, he could pick it up without anyone noticing.

Even though I knew Cannon knew about FA, I acted the same way toward him as if Sean had never told him.

From that point, I implemented an unspoken don't-ask-don't-tell policy. What I didn't know couldn't bother me, but Sean had to do what was right for him too. If trusting certain people to look out for me gave him peace of mind, that was his business. Cannon definitely needed to know since we were always together. That's when Maddie popped into my head. She probably should know too—but she should hear it from me.

Sean was what the girls called "hot," and because of his association with the athletes, he caught the upperclassman girls' interest. Cannon was into a fellow freshman girl, and during breaks from classes we'd all flirt shamelessly, explicitly teasing about the dance. We knew the dance could be a big night for us, when the flirting might turn into something more, like a date, or we'd at least find out if the girls liked us back. Still, I was a total chicken about going, mostly because dancing would expose my uncoordinated clumsy legs, and I was not very confident in my dancing abilities. My muscles would weaken significantly after standing for a while and after a long day of school. So by the dance that night, my legs would feel like Jell-O.

But Sean and Cannon had convinced me it would be dark enough that nobody would be staring, and they promised to craft ways for us to avoid the dance floor. If my crush did ask me to dance (which would be an excellent problem to have, right?), I'd ask her to take a walk instead.

As far as Cannon, Sean, and I were concerned, the dance theme was Divide and Conquer. We found the freshman girl group where Maddie and about fifteen other girls were standing, and we made our move. Cannon asked Ms. Cannon to go for a walk. Once she said yes, my courage soared, and Maddie agreed to take a walk with me too.

It was time. I knew I had to face my fears and come clean. If I didn't tell Maddie, she might think of her own reasons why I walked the way I did, like I was a stoner or a pill popper or something. I wanted to control my story, so the stakes were high. What if when I told her about FA, she stopped liking me, or worse, told all her friends? *No!* I wanted everyone to think I was The Man. I was afraid girls would put me in the friend zone, guys would call me weak, and my peers would laugh at me behind my back. And those were not even the worst things. I could've been branded the sad "sick kid" for the next four years.

My parents told my grade school teachers for me. Sean told Cannon for me. Now it was time for me to own it, own FA, and take a leap of faith that I could trust Maddie, which was scariest of all.

We sat down at a private area on the freshly cut grass under a thirty-foot oak tree on campus. I felt like I was walking toward a free-throw line in a tied championship game with no time left on the clock. I did not even think of missing, because that wasn't an option.

It was a dark Massachusetts fall night, and winds made it cool enough to wear a bulky sweatshirt. We voyaged to a shady area outside the biology building, where there were leaves in messy piles along the ground. We pushed away some of the leaves and planted ourselves on dry patches of dirt that had been impressed by the weight of the red, orange, and brown leaves. Even though the wind was making tree branches dance, I was sweating as if I'd run up and down a flight of stairs five times.

Now, I was alone with a girl I liked—capital letters LIKED— and I brainstormed. My goal was to tell her that even though I'd like to kiss her, she should know first that my hands and feet and legs don't work well.

Oh, yeah, that should seal the deal, Joe. That's totally what any actor like Jim or one in a romantic comedy would say!

Come to think of it, that *is* most likely what they would do.

Just say it, Joey. What's the worst thing that could happen? It's not like she'll fight you, right? I mean, she has never asked if there was something wrong, anyway.

I feel like Clark Kent.

JOE, SPIT IT OUT!

"Hey, umm, you, err, I have something to tell you."

Smooth, Joe, just like Jim Halpert.

I gulped in enough oxygen to roll out my spiel.

"So the real reason why Sean is an athlete and can run around a lot, and I do not, is that I can't. Well, I kinda can, but not really. Well, I can, but ..."

Maddie stopped me. "Joe, you're acting weird. Just spit it out, because I'm about to get up and go back to the dance."

"I have a disease that makes me walk differently. The disease is pretty complicated," I confessed.

That was all I was willing to tell Maddie about FA. I wanted to diminish it, turn it into a disease that means you don't play sports and that's about it. I didn't need to go into all the facts.

"I hope it doesn't bother you," I said.

I kicked the leaves around to keep from looking at Maddie.

"I honestly couldn't even tell," she said with a shy smile. Even if she was lying, I wanted this to be over already. "But I don't mind. I mean, you're still a normal kid, and I like you for you."

Wait, that's it? All my fear was shit. She didn't walk away and resent me? Wait, now we're making out?! Let's go!!!

Even though my relationship with Maddie only lasted for a few more months, I was still relieved. Since telling Maddie had gone so well, I went back and forth between thinking maybe telling other people would be more comfortable than I thought. Maybe people wouldn't judge me. But I didn't want things to change. Maddie was one person. If I added more people to the mix, the odds of someone treating me like a freak would increase. I decided that when things got terrible in a few years, I would tell people. But for now, I didn't need anyone else to know I had FA. According to Maddie, it was hard to notice.

Maybe it would be like this forever!

CHAPTER 11

Two-Face

Maddie was very cool about not telling anyone else my secret. Come to think of it, she was so relaxed about the whole thing. I figured nobody knew besides Sean, Maddie, and Cannon, because things didn't feel weird with other kids around school. Nobody suddenly went out of their way to carry my food tray or start opening doors for me.

My advisory group, the DI-bound athletes, were always rambunctious and lively. I loved messing around with them and vice versa. It was fascinating that even though they could have quickly pounded me into the ground like a pebble, they never did. Even when I would hide their backpacks from them or steal their pens, they remained calm. I would watch each of them maniacally scan the spaces between the lunch tables in search of their bags and wait until they would panic. At that moment, I would pop out of nowhere, pointing and laughing at them, with their backpack in my hand, and then stumble away from the cafeteria. Whenever they reciprocated, every time without fail, we'd all be laughing during the cat-and-mouse chase around the school, with me sometimes looking like a human pinball ricocheting off lockers and walls.

Like Jim from *The Office*, I decided I would keep my relationships with friends lighthearted. I wanted to make people laugh and be the friendly kid to my teachers while keeping people on their toes because of my antics. I wanted to be a chameleon, fitting in with all types of people. Fitting in became a job, all so I wouldn't stand out.

Being friendly and lively came naturally to me, but it still took a lot of energy to be charming and "Social Me." I was always on. Always ready with the right "What's up, my guy?" to greet the boys. Also in my arsenal were the casual "Hey, how are ya?" with a hug for the girls and the perfect self-deprecating joke about being a soccer manager instead of a player: "I'm hurt. But really, I'm just so talented, it would be unfair for me to play. I don't want to embarrass the others." Life as Social Me mixed with my secret life became a little exhausting.

When Social Me got home from school, I would shut down that version, and FA Me would take over. My feet would hurt from walking all day, and I would be in pain, exhausted. I felt like an eighty-year-old grandma who had multiple bunions on each foot. The only remedy would be to plant myself on my couch and do my homework while watching Paul Pierce and the Celtics dominate. If my mom told me dinner was ready, I'd rudely snap at her to bring it to me. After eating and completing the assignment for the next day, I'd muster any remaining energy to get up and go shower.

Showering was another chore. I sat on the tile floor so my legs wouldn't give out. Then, raising my arm to grab my shampoo was like shoulder-pressing a sixty-five-pound dumbbell. Getting back up in the shower was tough until my dad installed a grab bar I could hold onto to lift myself. After those debacles wrapped up and I stopped acting all pissed off, I would stumble into bed to get ready for the next day.

I felt as if I were both Clark Kent and Superman. Two-faced, living a double life. I preserved my energy and leg strength at home so I could again be a social butterfly the next day at school. At the same time, my parents were installing more grab bars and ADA-accessible bathrooms in the house. ADA stands for the Americans with Disabilities Act. That term is something I never thought I would have to know about.

My parents added multiple ramps to replace stairs around the house and widened bathrooms and hallways for wheelchairs, all while making sure everything was up to code per the ADA.

At school, Sean tried out for the varsity basketball team. Newcomers rarely made the team, but after his stellar tryout, Sean became the only freshman on the roster. His well-deserved achievement brought on more questions. It was that twin factor again. People couldn't grasp how one twin could be so dominant and athletically inclined, but the other voluntarily signed up to be a water boy. Because I loved basketball but no longer could play, I wasn't sure what after-school activity I could do. When I found out I could be a team manager—carrying equipment, filming the games, filling up water bottles, and fetching towels—I hopped on it.

When I sat on the bench during my eighth-grade season, I pretended to be a player-coach. Instead of aspiring to play like Kobe, I desired to coach like Mike Krzyzewski from Duke.

As the basketball team manager, one of my duties was to carry the bag of balls to each practice and game. The bag was heavy and challenging for me to carry. I struggled with its weight. I tried different ways to transport it without anyone noticing: dragging it behind me like a sled, throwing it over my shoulder like Santa Claus, and even taking some balls out and moving them in increments. After two weeks of watching me try and fail, my teammates began looking at me with guilt; they never asked me to carry anything again. That's when I knew it: SEAN. Again! I knew he'd told them. I chose to remain calm and play along. Even I had to admit it was pretty stupid to break my back on just one of the many responsibilities I had. Sean had adopted the role of keeper of my reputation, my very own PR machine.

When it came to basketball, Sean and I were in an entirely new league from what we'd known. The LA team looked like the U.S. Olympic team, consisting of multiple Division I athletes who were tall, strong, fast, and competitive. So instead of attempting to coach those with a much higher basketball IQ than I, I kept my mouth shut. That year, I just sat on the corner of the bench keeping the waters full, and I brought the team's favorite snacks on the bus to away games.

Although things at school were going well, I was deteriorating physically, and mentally I felt like a ticking timebomb. My fear of telling people about my disability, that I suffer from a neurological disorder, had taken root like a giant in-grown zit that never goes away. You can try to pop it, but it always comes back.

I saw athletes every day, which motivated me to exercise in LA's weight room. I needed to own my physical game to play the best defense I could against FA. I kept my fear of FA's progression quiet and remained Mr. Positive at school and Mr. Pessimist at home.

The doctor appointments throughout my high school years would always be disappointing. Since there was no treatment, they just monitored me. My doctors measured the amount of progression, based on my last six-month visit, to see where my body was declining. Because there is no cure for FA, I could not be prescribed any medicine or remedy. Doctors just advised me to eat healthfully and avoid foods that would cause inflammation in my body. The doctors then would tell me to exercise, which my new giant friends already had taken care of.

I was still walking unassisted, but with a limp. I was a keen observer and could locate inconspicuous things to grab onto when I needed to. I used grab bars to walk around my house and had strengthened my arms from working out. If I'd walk a lot during the day and my legs gave out, I usually was strong enough to catch myself and not hit the floor. Don't get me wrong: I did find myself on the ground from time to time, unable to get up, and it's hard to come back from that. When there was nothing to grab onto when I walked, my trouble became noticeable, so I became hyper-focused on making sure that didn't happen. It's a lot to keep at the top of your mind when you try to act like Mr. Cool all the time.

To everyone at school, it looked as if I were doing great. I was the happy-go-lucky kid everyone loves to be around. Outside of school and home, my world consisted of people who stared at me, judged me based on my appearance, and thought I was drunk all the time. I was too afraid to go to the mall, to movie theaters, or to any public area with my friends or family.

I happen to love going to the food court at the mall and getting a soft pretzel from Auntie Anne's. You know who else loves going to the food court at the mall and getting a soft pretzel from Auntie Anne's? A ton of people. You know who stares at me like I'm an alien? That same ton of people.

Not only did I live a double life, but my life became a series of contradictions. Pulling off a casual "random" hangout with friends required lots of not-so-random pregame strategy. I learned to have a game plan to seem unplanned. A "Hey, wanna hang out after school?" filled my mind with essential questions:

Who would be there?

Could I trust them?

Did I know the layout of someone's house?

How many stairs were there, both inside and outside?

Was the driveway on an incline?

Who were their parents, and will they call me out for my unbalanced walk?

Then, I had to worry about whether we were going to leave the house once we got there. If at least one of the questions asked had an answer that made me feel uncomfortable, then I wouldn't go. I would just lie and say I had a stomachache or a migraine, or that I had to stay home with my sick dog.

When I put Social Me away and replaced him with FA Me, I'd sit home and play NBA 2K on my Xbox. But deep down, I would have the worst case of FOMO. I would always get jealous of seeing other kids my age going out and having fun, not having to give a second thought to any of it. I was afraid if I went with them, I'd wind up a bystander to something they wanted to do, like riding bikes, playing ball, or going to the mall. I tried super hard not to be seen as handicapped, but I was disabling myself even more.

CHAPTER 12

Cruel Summer

Like many kids, I love the summer—no school, no homework, and barely any worries. In Massachusetts, winters are freezing and it's dark outside by 4:30 p.m., so you hardly see anyone. FA makes winter even worse.

FA affects how well blood circulates in my body. For the average person, blood moves well throughout the body, keeping their joints, muscles, and ligaments moving swiftly. When blood circulates well, that person doesn't get cold too quickly. A person without FA can feel their lower limbs and, well, they generally don't feel like they've been sitting in the ice cream man's van for the entire day.

Have you ever gone outside in the winter without proper gear, and your hands or ears turn white or bright red or both before they go numb? That happens to me daily, so I am uncomfortably cold from my waist to my toes all year-round. It's almost unbearable in the winter here, when it's already so cold to begin with.

The first time I noticed it was at a high school football game. It was late November, a sunny day but also cold and windy. The majority of the crowd was wearing pants and heavy coats.

They also kept warm by shaking their bodies, jumping up and down, and walking up and down the bleachers. I was envious of their ability to move around that way. I was so cold, it became physically painful. I tried, to no avail, using those instant hand and toe warmers you pick up at Walgreens; my mom used to use them when she was watching me play lacrosse. During the game, I even considered ordering a pair of UGG boots.

It's not uncommon in Massachusetts for temperatures to stay below twenty-five degrees for months at a time. Even if I wear a puffy winter coat, a snow hat and gloves, snow pants, and warm Timberland boots, I'm still freezing. My doctor said that if it ever hits below ten degrees, I need to stay inside in a heated area or else my body will "shut off." Not sure what that means, but I'm making it my mission to keep it from happening.

When you are from New England, the first spring day above fifty-five degrees is magical! Then, the summers are warm, and all we want to do is lie on the beach and get our tans on while listening to "Toes" by Zac Brown Band on a portable speaker.

Since Sean and I lived in Central Massachusetts but almost all our friends from LA lived in Eastern Massachusetts near the Boston area, we didn't see each other much over the summer. The forty-five-minute drive from our house to theirs was long. It was too far to ask our parents for a ride. That made summer a great time to hang with our original best friends from St. Anna's, who all lived close to Sean and me.

Growing up, during the days, we swam at one of our pools. We played endless pool basketball, Marco Polo, and games off the diving board. Our parents would still be at work, so we'd become in charge of the house. (Although that might sound dangerous, we were all good kids, so there was never an issue.) Most of the time, we were at Petey's house because of his great pool and the backyard with that magical basketball court.

On rainy days, we would still hang out and play Call of Duty. Petey had a headset connected, so we'd just sit around talking smack to other online players. On the warm, dry nights, we walked down the street to grab soft-serve at our local ice cream shop. We would get either the cookie dough raspberry ice cream with sprinkles and graham crackers, called the Sweetness Deluxe, or the Oreo shortcake sundae. The warmer the days, the more fun and the more incredible.

One of my absolute favorite things about summer was swimming. The heat was scorching and none of us had summer jobs yet, so we could swim every day. And as horrible as winter's cold conditions were on my body, the water was a welcome friend. I loved swimming, although Michael Phelps would never call what I do "swimming." But I could walk more easily in the water, and the motion of swimming was good exercise for me because it added little stress on my body. I could stand up and easily walk around *by myself!* The pool water was as high as my sternum, so the water acted as a spotter for my wobbly legs. It was such a relief to be in the pool, because I couldn't quite keep up with my buddies in the more aggressive, physical backyard games. I couldn't wait to relive those summer days again.

The summer going into my sophomore year was challenging and eye-opening. Where I'm from, almost every high school athlete works just as hard in the offseason as they do during the season. Although Sean's basketball season was over, baseball season was under way. Baseball was Sean's second love. By the age of fifteen, he'd slimmed down and stood about five-nine. He was such a fantastic shortstop; he made LA's varsity team as a freshman and our county's summer baseball travel team. Three of our other hometown best friends played football for their high schools. Although it wasn't football season yet, they had to participate daily in captain's practice, weightlifting sessions, team workouts, and sprint drills. Jon, the hockey player, wanted to be the best, so he had to train like the best. So, he either worked out or skated every day—sometimes both. Bella, my cousin, spent her offseason from lacrosse splitting time between training and working as a lifeguard.

That meant that on numerous ninety-degree days, there was me. I was just waiting for one of my friends to have free time so I could hang out with them. At fifteen, I couldn't play sports. I worked out a few days a week, but not like a bodybuilding maniac on the beaches of California.

I did try working as a busboy at my mom's best friend's restaurant. But since I kept stumbling over my own feet, it wasn't a good fit. After cleaning a table, I had to walk thirty feet to bring the dirty utensils, bread baskets, glasses, and plates back to the kitchen.

Me + Carrying Valuables = Disaster.

I broke so many of the restaurant's items that it cost more to replace them than I could ever make in tips. One of the managers, who was very sweet but demanded excellence from all employees, saw me trip over myself and fall into a bunch of condiments, creating a mess of ketchup, mustard, and mayonnaise all over the floor. I held my breath as she approached, figuring she'd yell at me, but instead, she just said kindly, "It's an accident. I'll clean it up. No worries." I took her kindness as a dead giveaway that she, and probably the whole restaurant staff, knew my secret, and I didn't have Sean to blame this time. I knew my mom's friend would never fire me, so I voluntarily quit. I wanted there to be enough plates!

This was my first real summer in high school with FA on the forefront, and it hurt. I saw the difference between this summer and all the summers before. I couldn't play basketball or Wiffle ball with my friends anymore. Pool basketball had gotten too physical for me, so I sat out. Sometimes on weekends, when parents were around, they'd sit with me on the side. I would listen to them talk about their lives, but I always kept wishing I was somewhere else, that I didn't have to make small talk with Mrs. Anthony about how her knees didn't work very well anymore and desperately needed replacements.

With no job, only limited pool time with friends, and no sports to play with the rest of the crew, I counted down the days to our family vacation. That August, when my older siblings' summer internships had ended and Sean's summer baseball was over, our parents took us on vacation. We all loved the warm weather and preferred being on a beach. One year my parents took us to Aruba. If you've ever been to Aruba, you know it's an island worth visiting.

Aruba, also known as One Happy Island, is small and thrives off tourism. The island has many resorts lining the shoreline from one end to the other, with bars and restaurants overlooking the ocean. We loved our first trip so much we decided to go back a few years later. I knew I'd need a wheelchair not only to get around the island, but to get through the airport.

The trip would be the first time I'd been in a wheelchair since "the summer of the cyst." Based on what I remembered about that summer, I feared this trip to Aruba would be one I hated. It wasn't so much that my parents told me to use the wheelchair because they thought I'd trip over myself or something. It was all the other crazy people who scared them. I didn't want to wait for hours at the TSA checkpoint, so I figured the wheelchair might help us all through that more quickly—a "perk" of wheelchair travel.

As soon as my family got to the airport, an attendant spotted Kaela in her scooter and me in my wheelchair. He checked us right in. He walked us all to the front of the crowded security line. Since I couldn't balance myself standing for twenty seconds, the body scanners—the ones that make you stand with your arms over your head like the police are frisking you—weren't going to work. I had to get a private pat-down the old-fashioned way. I get that TSA is just doing their job, but they could've been a little gentler and maybe even a teeny bit friendlier about getting all up in my *private* business. Then, they had to rub down my entire wheelchair as well. During this whole scene, which was entirely out in the open, everyone stared at me. I kind of understood it, like when you see a family fighting in a crowded area and you know you shouldn't look, but you do.

Once the "private" screening ended, I left my pride somewhere in Terminal 1 and rejoined my family, who, besides Kaela, had been waiting patiently for several minutes. The gate agent called for us both on the microphone and allowed us to board the plane before anyone else. To get on the flight, we had to use the airline's wheelchairs, which are like straitjackets on wheels, built to fit through the aisles of the plane. The attendants strapped us in, and there was no possible way we could move our bodies. I hated getting in one, but it worked and got me to my seat. The staff wheeled me down to my seat as my mom followed. The staff members were two women, so I acted calm and cool. During the transfer, each woman grabbed one of my arms. I purposely flexed both biceps to try to get a compliment.

I got nothing, but shooters shoot.

Once we landed, Aruba was immediately sunny, warm, and peaceful. The wheelchair was so helpful, because now I didn't have to worry about getting too tired to walk or carry things, or about falling and embarrassing myself. I didn't have to use my energy on figuring out how to get around. I just focused on swimming and sitting on the beach.

Although I couldn't legally gamble, there are many casinos in Aruba where kids can go in with their families but cannot play. Ryan, who had just turned twenty-two, could gamble, so he took Sean and me with him. I loved to watch him play blackjack, and on this occasion, there were only two other people at the table, so the dealer allowed Sean and me to sit at the table and watch.

Sean and Ryan helped transfer me out of my wheelchair and onto a seat where I could see the high blackjack table. While we were there, a woman walked up and stood behind her fiancé, seated next to Ryan. It was evident that she'd had a few drinks; she was very chatty and slurring her words as she tried to befriend everyone at the table. We were all talking it up for a while before she spied my wheelchair.

"Whose wheelchair?" she asked.

"Oh, it's mine," I said, smiling.

"Yeah, okay, right. No, whose is it really?"

I quickly looked over at Ryan.

"It's really his," Ryan said tactfully before changing the subject.

But the woman kept glancing over without saying anything, looking confused as she would pan to the wheelchair and then to me. After a few more hands, my brothers and I wanted to leave, so Ryan and Sean helped me back into my wheelchair. The woman watched, covered her face, and ran away from the table in the opposite direction. She fled like I was the sun and I was going to blind her. Although I brushed it off and tried to enjoy the rest of my trip, that debacle wouldn't leave my mind.

It made me realize that some people have a way of thinking about disabled people. They talk loudly when our hearing works just fine, speak slowly as if we don't understand English, or look at us as though we just landed here from Mars. I thought about how those people believe that physically disabled people should look a certain way. They expect you to be old or limbless, to have a cast on, or to have some physical proof that, yes, you need a wheelchair.

Can you just be an average teenage kid, laughing and making foolish jokes with people who aren't disabled?

I realize the woman was drunk and had no malicious intentions, but I just kept thinking about how this kind of reaction might be my new reality. Would strangers ask similar questions for the rest of my life? If so, I would have to formulate responses to control others' reactions—or to control my reaction to them. I thought these quick answers felt unnecessarily burdensome. It was a lot of work, all to make *other people* feel better about their shortsightedness.

Now I was responsible for them and me?

It was the first summer in history that I couldn't wait to go back to school.

CHAPTER 13

Hello, Darkness, My Old Friend

As a sports family, we all watched sports all the time. From the late spring through early fall, the Red Sox were always on the television throughout the house, even when nobody was watching. From the early fall through the late winter, the Patriots became a seventh family member. From the late fall through spring, I'd watch the Celtics or Bruins. If games ever overlapped, we'd have one game on in one room and the other game on in the other room. From David Ortiz to Tom Brady to Paul Pierce to Patrice Bergeron, we Boston fans felt lucky, year after year.

One NFL Sunday, my buddies and I got to go to Gillette Stadium to watch our beloved Patriots. Going was so huge that when my friends were planning the trip, I decided to take all my usual worries and anxiety and throw them out the window.

Pats game in Foxborough? TB12? Are you kidding me?! There was no "stomachache" in the world that would keep me from watching Tom Brady throw a perfect spiral in real life.

My dream the night before was unusual. Instead of my normal dreams of hitting the lottery, getting the girl, or winning the big game, I do the opposite. I am pitching for the Boston Red Sox. We're playing my town's JV softball team. It's Game 7 of the World Series, we are winning by two runs, there are two outs, and the final batter is up with the bases loaded. The count is three balls and two strikes. My middle school girlfriend, Katie S., who is still mad at me for breaking up with her at recess, is the potential third out. Fans at Fenway Park are going crazy and can taste the championship. Next pitch, I try to throw my dominant, ninety-nine-mile-per-hour fastball. But during my windup, I slip and end up throwing a thirty-mile-per-hour eephus pitch down the middle. Katie hits the ball and it goes out of the park, out of Boston, and out of the country. I've blown it. I begin crying on the mound as Katie points at me and laughs while running the bases. Angry Sox fans run at me with pitchforks. Then, I awaken.

The next day, we arrived at the stadium. I was so pumped with adrenaline that I didn't notice the mile-long walk from our parking spot into the stadium, then up several flights of stairs. As we watched the Pats dominate, all the screaming, cheering, and jumping up and down in the stands taxed my body. (There were probably a few man-hugs in the mix, too.)

Leaving the stadium to walk to our car, I crashed like I was coming off a sugar high. Everyone was still trading stories and play-by-play when I went mute. I was too tired to talk. Then I realized I was walking arm in arm with my buddies linked to me on either side like a chain, holding me up, making our way back to the car. They must have known about FA, but I needed all the help I could get, so I didn't care about who had told them.

Our slower pace caused some chaos as we were funneling through the aisles of the parking lot. We heard voices snarling, "Hurry up, kid!" "What the hell is going on?" "Move it, asshole!"

It was their world, and I was just in it, being a nuisance.

These remarks upset me, and my buddies wanted to do something about it. I had to act like it was no big deal to keep the peace.

CHAPTER 14

A Not-So-Sweet Sixteen

The scarcer something is, the more valuable it becomes. Massachusetts weather is drastically different during each season of the year. Regardless of the chilly weather, the fall is beautiful. Leaves are changing colors, and the hills and mountains are a patchwork of orange, red, yellow, and green.

Of course, fall also brings the return to school. When you're a kid, going back to school after almost three months is nerve-racking. Not just because it means the end of twelve-hour TV binges, but because you know you're different than you were in June—and people will notice.

We're in school for roughly ten months, or forty weeks. When you don't see someone every day for twelve weeks, you notice the changes when you do see them again: the growth spurts, the haircuts, the new facial hair, the deeper voices. I remember the first time the differences in my classmates were noticeable. It was the first day of seventh grade, and everyone seemed a little taller with a little less baby fat. We'd gone from playing four square at recess to lamenting over our MySpace profile pictures in just twelve weeks!

Heading into sophomore year, it seemed like since my classmates were physically growing up and becoming more robust, they were more confident in themselves. I wanted—no, *needed*—some of that. The only significant change I boasted in September was a sunburn from my trip to Aruba. I swore I saw some armpit hair, so I bragged to my mom about it. She looked more closely and nicked it from my smooth, bare pit, laughing that it was a tick I had gotten from being outside watching my buddies play.

Even though I stood a respectable five-six, everyone else my age still seemed to look more mature than I did. Even the kids who were shorter than I was somehow looked older than me.

While my friends seemed to be coming into themselves, I was losing parts of myself: my speech, my energy, and my ability to balance. My physical decline resulted in more slurring and spitting when I spoke and falling over my own two feet when I walked, mostly when I was more tired than usual. Instead of naturally talking to a friend as we walked to the cafeteria or class, I had to focus on those verbal exchanges. And the nonverbal ones too. A fist bump could become a punch in the chest; a bro hug could end up looking like I was trying to suck a friend's neck. If someone ever saw me topple over in an attempt to say hello, I would do what I did best and make myself the brunt of the joke. "Damn growing pains" was my usual save. Incidents like the embarrassed drunk woman in the Aruba casino and the Pats game became more frequent. Patterns of social awkwardness emerged, and I became overly sensitive and paranoid about it.

Sophomore year, my Leominster and LA buddies and I focused more on partying. On weekend nights, it was pretty much the only fun thing to do. Instead of the old routine of meeting girls at the movie theater on Friday nights and maybe holding their hand for one minute, we went to a party at someone's house. For me, too much partying (i.e., drinking) made it even harder to speak clearly and walk without falling, but that never stopped me. When we drank, everyone else slurred and stumbled, too. Dysfunctional as it was, we were equals. Drinking was when I really "fit in."

We slick sixteen-year-olds thought we were pulling one over on our parents, but pretty much most of the adults were on to us. Some parents were cool about it. They figured that since we were going to do it anyway, they'd have us do it under their roof where nobody was allowed to leave and each parent was in contact with the other. Some parents even admitted that they used to do the same thing when they were our age. But others—like my class-mate Rachel Smyth's parents—were not having it.

Ironically, it was Rachel's parents who were throwing one of the most talked-about parties of the year: Rachel's Sweet Sixteen. Rachel's parents were not fond of the idea of thirty kids drunk at their home (which makes sense now, but at the time seemed ridiculous). They made it clear there would be no alcohol and that they would not tolerate any funny business. Rachel texted everyone multiple times repeating these conditions, along with the warning that if her parents even smelled alcohol, they would shut down the party and Rachel would be grounded until she went to college. She then added a little incentive by reminding us all, "My aunt's a Statie, and she will be at the party."

Dude, I don't know if I want to go if a state trooper will be there!

My buddies and I went to Rachel's house anyway. We didn't even consider pregaming, but still, my walking made me look like I had been at a dive bar all day. My buddies holding me up as we rang the doorbell was a bad look. Rachel's parents opened the door and scanned us like they were TSA agents, and my mood tanked. Rachel's parents didn't crack a smile. I gave her dad what I thought was my firmest, manliest, most grownup handshake, because I thought it would endear me to him, except he squeezed twice as hard as I could. The warnings Rachel had texted clearly were no joke. Her dad's stare-down was overkill.

My friends and I went in and saw Aunt Statie, donned in street clothes with glasses, her badge pinned to her pants pocket. She wore a Massachusetts State Police hat and marched around the kitchen island as we filled our cups with Sprite. I tried to loosen up, telling myself little reminders like, "You have nothing to hide, Joe," and, "Just have fun." So my buddies and I began talking to everyone. When the song "Where Them Girls At" by David Guetta came on, almost everyone started dancing. Not me, though. Instead, I found a space in the corner and socialized with the other non-dancers. Throughout the party, some kids danced, some talked, and all took photos to post on Facebook. Rachel's parents allowed us to play beer pong with cups of water. I never had to pee so much in my life, but I was too afraid to leave my spot.

By the end of the party, I was physically spent. Standing around all night had made my balance worse than it had been when I arrived. When Petey went to the bathroom, I decided to follow him because I needed a plus-one to support me wherever I went. Rachel's aunt had a hawk's eye and followed us. She stood about ten feet behind us in the kitchen and just stared at me the whole time, without saying a word. From the way she was folding her arms and glaring, I could tell she thought I was drunk. I had developed a sixth sense for body language. Petey could have been wearing the invisibility cloak from *Harry Potter* for all Aunt Statie knew. Thankfully, she eventually walked away from us.

But when we came back toward the party ...

"Excuse me," Rachel's aunt said as she saw us walking into the kitchen, "please come outside."

Despite the hand gesture directing me toward the door, Petey began to follow me.

"Just him. Alone," she said, pointing at me, her wide eyes magnified by her thick glasses.

Like a scared kindergartener saying goodbye to his parents on the first day of school, I reluctantly parted ways with Petey. I walked with the aunt to the front door to head outside, panicking. It felt like the house was pounding along with my racing heart. As Aunt Statie walked behind me, probably anticipating the way it would look when she handcuffed me outside, I saw Rachel's parents monitoring the other side of the party. This pre-arrest disaster seemed like a setup from *Punk'd*, but why would Ashton Kutcher be in Central Massachusetts at a Sweet Sixteen to prank *me*, anyway?

SHIT, SHIT, SHIT, JOE. JUST RUN AWAY.

Can't do that, neither theoretically nor physically. Even if I had been able to pull a Forrest Gump, burst out of my leg braces, and run from the bully, it would have signaled that I had something to hide.

My only option was surrender. The light on the front porch was solar bright and tilted toward my eyes, making it hard for me to see Aunt Statie, like she was behind a one-way mirror in an interrogation room. She cut right to the chase.

"And just about how drunk are you?" she asked.

I stood there like a zombie, which probably confirmed her beliefs.

"No, no way! No, ab-absolutely not, madam (slur), uhhh, ma'am. I, uhhh, can't walk, well, (slur), I mean, I can, but uhhh ..."

Typically I relied on others to explain my peculiarities. I was on my own here, alone with FA. I searched for a better answer and dug deep, the *Jeopardy!* music on loop in my head.

"I'M HANDICAPPED!" I yelled, as if I'd miraculously thought of the right answer to a *Wheel of Fortune* puzzle just before the buzzer went off.

"Wait, what? You shouldn't joke about that!" Aunt Statie exclaimed as I looked at her. She clearly did not catch my drift.

I'd assumed the "H" word would save the day here, but now we were going into a new bit. She stood there silently, but her gaze was no longer deadly. Her brows were like shapeshifters changing from angry zigzag to furrowed and perplexed. Thankfully, Petey stayed close behind (just like good parents do on the first day of kindergarten), watching the whole encounter through the living room window. After my failed attempt to save myself, he came to the rescue.

Oddly, Rachel's aunt seemed relieved that Petey didn't mind his business. She listened intently as he explained that I was indeed handicapped and suffered from a rare disease affecting my balance—the whole saga. As Petey protected my honor and reputation, I just stared down at my ripped jeans like a pitiable fool. I knew this was my new normal and that as I grew older, my normal would be impossible to outrun, attached to me like my shadow. I never liked my shadow, by the way. Instead, I wanted to stomp on it whenever the sun hit the sidewalk at the right time of day.

There is an intrusion that comes along with telling people you have an illness. When you share that information with someone, you're letting them close to your inner conflicts, fears, and vulnerabilities. Imagine someone reading your diary every day. That's what it felt like every time someone knew about FA. There is very little privacy allowed when everyone can see the parts you hate the most about yourself. Now, imagine having to go around justifying how you talk, how you walk, the way you think, the way you eat, the way you sit, stand, dance, or don't dance. Imagine everywhere you go, people asking you, *Why are you the way you are?* At sixteen years old, I had to make excuses for myself and answer inane questions. Then I had to explain my actions to people who didn't realize their questions felt like punches right to my face.

After Petey explained to Aunt Statie what was going on, she felt terrible and begged us to stay. It didn't undo the adrenaline rush that made me feel lightheaded. Petey, my best friend to this day, could see I was exhausted. "Brush it off," he told me. There was no way I could do that, though. We went back to the party to join our friends, and I tried to enjoy myself, but I couldn't. A little later, we all left and crashed at Petey's house. Besides Petey, nobody knew what had happened. I acted as if we had just been to any other Sweet Sixteen.

The major gossip that came out of the party was that Tyler T. made out with Michele that night—in Rachel's parents' bedroom. Yet I'd been judged to be one of the bad seeds, like the ones who break curfew, smoke weed, steal money from their mom's pocketbook, or sneak into strangers' garages to chase vodka with Red Bull. I did not want to be seen like that, but it didn't matter what I wanted. I would never have the power to control other people's judgments or versions of me. Not unless FA became my preamble.

CHAPTER 15

Black Mamba

There are two things on a sixteen-year-old boy's mind: girls and getting a driver's license. Driving, especially driving alone, means independence, and just the thought of it is exciting. Of course, it also means it's time to start acting more mature.

Do you know what the Latin translation of the word "sopho-more" is? *Sophos* means wise, and *moros* means both foolish and dull. In my opinion, the ancient Romans were telling future genera-tions that when you're a sophomore, you're a wise but immature idiot with a lot to learn.

Looking back, that was the perfect way to describe my home-town friend group. When we weren't playing Call of Duty, swim-ming in someone's pool, or eating whatever we wanted (because we were young and could eat a medium Number Ten meal from Wendy's twice a day with no repercussions), we were talking about cars.

Our parents had always been there to drive us everywhere. All of our families had multiple children, so pretty much every parent had a large car. Over time, our parents created an excel-lent carpool system. But as we all got closer to sixteen, the legal driving age in Massachusetts, we grew increasingly envious of the freedom we saw in our older schoolmates who could drive them-selves around. They were going to Dunkin' to grab an iced coffee whenever they wanted, and they could go two hours away to the beaches of Cape Cod to enjoy the summer sun. It made us itch for our turn. All we could think about was getting our licenses, while praying our parents would give us our older siblings' beat-up cars.

But once again, I was different. I knew my legs and feet weren't strong enough to use the foot pedals, so the thought of driving scared me. Knowing I would be dependent on everyone else got me down too, and of course there would be the twin factor again, as always. I knew I could get my license because Kaela had gotten hers, but I didn't know how she drove.

I'm sure my sister was not happy she had to be the FA guinea pig for me, but I certainly was grateful she'd paved the way. Everything I worried or wondered about, she'd already had to deal with.

Once I turned fifteen and a half, I was eligible to begin taking a driver's education course. There are two components: the classroom instruction and the actual, real-life driving part.

For five straight Saturdays from 9 a.m. to 3 p.m., I sat in a classroom with Sean and thirty other almost-sixteen-year-olds I didn't know. We watched vehicle-safety videos and car wreck re-enactments with crash test dummies and unsuspecting pedestrians showing us the dangers of texting while driving.

One day, I had to go to class without Sean, who was excused for a baseball game. The instructor discussed the many dangers of drunk driving. To demonstrate, he passed around a pair of drunk-goggles, which looked like they were part of a plastic snorkeling set you buy in the beach aisle at Target. The idea was for each of us to put them on and walk around to experience how dangerous drunk driving would be. I watched my fellow classmates bang into desks, turn in circles like dogs chasing their tails, fail to find an open door, and scribble their names when trying to write them on a smartboard. Simple activities like walking in a straight line, standing on one leg, grabbing car keys from the table, or tossing a small ball became impossible. Everyone else was laughing and smiling, but knowing I would have to take part in this experiment freaked me out. I already walked like I had drunk-goggles on, and I wasn't sure how further impairing my pre-existing impairment would turn out. I had to think fast now that the goggles were being passed to me.

"Um, sir?" I said to the instructor. "When I last did this in my health class at school, I wound up spraining my thumb."

All eyes were on me as my lie floated around the room.

"Well, we wouldn't want that to happen here," the instructor said. He was patient and turned my lie into a truth. "I'm sure that is a lesson in itself that you will never forget about how dangerous drunk driving is."

To my great relief, he gestured to me to pass the goggles to the next kid.

Finally, after weeks of missing out on watching afternoon NCAA football games, those pointless Saturdays were over. It was time to put the pedal to the metal, except not in the way everyone else typically does.

First, I had to get a learning permit in order to drive with an instructor. In Massachusetts, you can take the computerized test when you turn sixteen. So on our birthday, October 4, Sean and I went to the DMV after school. To pass the test, you need eighteen correct answers to twenty-one questions. During the exam, I answered two of the first fifteen wrong. After every wrong answer, I screamed, "Shit!" Sean was sitting next to me, fifteen-for-fifteen by then, dying laughing. As the stakes got higher with each question I got wrong, I began to sweat and fidget. I answered the next three correctly. Then question number nineteen asked,

"What do white painted curbs mean?" I had no idea. *No parking? First responders only? People over fifty-five? School bus parking?* I guessed and chose B.

Wrong.

I stormed out of the building, fuming, and waited in my mom's car while Sean took his permit photo. As angry as I was, I went back to the DMV the next day, passed, and cheesed so hard in my photo. I was so excited to learn how to drive.

I had one-on-one instruction with Jeff, a seventy-some-thing-year-old man with a cane, who limped up to my driveway after school one day. Jeff wore raggedy construction boots and jeans, plus a brown coat with a Vietnam War battle patch on the right arm. He also wore a cool military hat. Jeff came over every Tuesday and Thursday afternoon, and sometimes on Saturday mornings, for four hours over eight weeks. We would drive all over Leominster together. As I learned to make left turns and three-point turns, Jeff would tell me stories about his life. He often began with, "Back in my day..."

Jeff had a heart of gold. He cared about me passing my road test and wanted to see me achieve some independence. I needed twenty-four hours of driving instruction before I could take my test, and during all of them, Jeff taught me how to use the special hand controls attached to the steering wheel. These would act as my pedals so I could brake and accelerate with my hands instead of my feet. Due to his age, Jeff was also unable to drive using foot pedals. He was an expert at showing me how to train my brain to make the hand actions second nature. We drove around town in Jeff's silver 1990 Cadillac. It was a regular car that anybody could drive. When I drove, I covered the foot pedals with a metal shield so my foot wouldn't accidentally slip onto the brake or the accelerator.

The steering wheel was the same as in every car, except an eight-inch-long lever stuck out of it on the bottom left. That lever controlled the acceleration and the brake. To brake, I pushed the lever forward. To accelerate, I pulled it toward myself. Hand controls leave a driver only one free hand for steering. At about 1:30 on the steering wheel, there's a round ball, nicknamed a suicide knob. (I don't know why it's called that.) When I grabbed it, it would help my right hand leverage the wheel better and turn it faster. Only Kaela, a selection of large trucks, and tractors used a suicide knob … and now I did, too.

When test day arrived, I felt lucky that Jeff would accompany me along with the examiner who would decide to fail me or pass me. Word on the street was that my examiner was notorious for failing kids. I was a hypocrite for thinking that because I was going for a "special" driver's license, maybe my examiner would take some pity on me. In my off-road life, I wanted to keep FA a secret, but on the road, when up against a guy who just wants to ruin a kid's day, I wanted all the help I could get.

My examiner made me parallel park, back up fifty feet straight, and make a few left turns. He talked constantly about the weather, the potholes, and his kids. I'm pretty sure that was his way of testing my ability to stay focused and keep my eyes on the road. He couldn't have known that Jeff was always yapping about something, so I'd learned how to drive and talk simultaneously from day one. The exam lasted fifteen minutes. Jeff never said a word.

"Okay, bring her home," the examiner said. I parked the car in the same spot where we'd started. There was silence for the first time since I'd buckled my seatbelt. I could hear the pen's scribbling sounds against his clipboard (such a power move!). And then, finally, the official words.

"Yeah. Sure. I'll pass that."

I had just assumed I would get Kaela's car, a 2000 black Mercury Sable, as a hand-me-down because it was already equipped with hand controls. Once Kaela began using a motorized scooter permanently, my parents bought her an old minivan equipped with hand controls, a suicide knob, and an automatic ramp. The Sable had been good to Kaela, and its compact size was perfect for her five-foot frame. But I could not imagine how my extra inches of height would allow me to squeeze into the driver's seat. Getting my lanky, weak legs into a crouching position in that car was like fitting that extra pair of shoes into your overpacked luggage. With enough shoving and bending, you can make it work, but it's not ideal.

To my surprise, my parents got me a black 2008 Jeep Grand Cherokee with a teal interior. It was large, with five seats and a big trunk, and it sat up higher than the Sable, which helped me get in and move around more easily. Sure, it didn't look or drive like a Ferrari, but I felt just as cool in it.

Having a wicked cool car would not be enough, though. I needed to give the Jeep a personality, an identity, something legends are made of—legends like Kobe Bryant. So I honored him by calling the Jeep the Black Mamba, Kobe's nickname. Since I was permitted to park my car closest to my teachers' buildings, I could stare at my beautiful Mamba through the window all day long.

I christened the Mamba with a trip to none other than the Dunkin' drive-through to get Coolattas with Sean. As I reached out the window to grab the drink holder from the drive-through attendant, I dropped it—no surprise, thanks to FA. The Coolattas went flying, hit the ground, and splashed all over the side of my Mamba.

"It's good luck," Sean said before I turned to the attendant, my face beet-red, and apologized profusely. We laughed the whole way home without our refreshing iced beverages. I don't think we needed the caffeine anyway.

Getting my driver's license meant I also got my first handicapped placard, which would've been helpful at that Pats game a year earlier. But I would not have used it at the stadium, and I did not use it now. I hid the pass like it was a scarlet letter. All the attention people gave the immaculate Black Mamba would have been negated by the stigma of being a handicapped driver.

What was the point of the Mamba if I had to hang a giant blue wheelchair tag from the rearview mirror?

I could imagine what the kids at school would say as I turned the corner onto campus all decked out like I'm some mafia superstar with a tag that screamed, I CAN PARK WHEREVER I WANT BECAUSE I'M WEAK AND MY LIFE IS HARD. I might as well have my mom drop me off at the front of school and wipe dirt off my face with her finger.

I begged my parents not to get me a placard in the first place, but legally I had to have one if I wanted to drive. Wow, the state of Massachusetts just thought of *everything*. Even though I didn't want to tell people about FA, I had to have proof for the police so that, if something terrible were to happen, they could know my impaired speech and walking had nothing to do with drugs or alcohol.

I had to figure out ways of getting to school before everyone else or removing the pass from my dashboard at lightning speed and stuffing it into my glove box. I didn't want the other kids to see. In my mind, people tend to think there is something wrong with your brain even when it's just your body that is the problem. Then, they talk to you like you're slow or deaf. It's quite the phenomenon that happens to this day. All I had were my brains, so I needed to defend them at all costs.

Although the pass brought me anxiety, getting it was the right thing to do. And it actually was very convenient, especially during the New England winters.

With the Black Mamba, big blue wheelchair placard or not, life was going to get interesting.

CHAPTER 16

Coach Kev's History Class

At different times of the day, as many teachers as kids stroll through high school hallways. You have the teachers who drool over history, poetry, or anatomy as if it were a triple chocolate hot fudge sundae. You've got the drill sergeant types running their classrooms with the sole mission of breaking students by handing out detention slips. There are the new teachers who act like your best friend one minute, then threaten a meeting with your parents the next. And you have those inspirational types who use movement like skilled interpretive dancers as they reenact an excerpt from a Broadway play.

One of my favorite teachers, Coach Kev, was a cross between Harry Potter's Dumbledore, because it seemed like there was nothing he couldn't do, and *Boy Meets World's* Mr. Feeny, who never directly gives you the correct answer but guides you in the right direction to find it yourself. Coach Kev, as we called him, was never afraid to tell it like it is: "There are no stupid questions, just stupid answers." Coach Kev not only taught history but also coached LA's varsity basketball team. As a teacher and coach, he knew every student's name, even if they were an extra in the school play.

Sean and I were with Coach Kev a lot during basketball season. Sean was a starter on the team by then, and I enjoyed being the manager. I was hanging on by a thread to stay involved with a sport I desperately loved. Because we spent so much time with Coach Kev during practices, at games, and traveling to tournaments with

Kev's wife and three children, our families bonded. We trusted him as part of our inner circle, and therefore, my parents told him my FA secret during my freshman year.

I was excited that I would finally have Coach Kev in a classroom setting for an elective history course about the Cuban Missile Crisis. I could just relax in this class and put in enough effort to make Coach Kev happy. It was a huge relief.

By this time, my walking had gotten significantly worse, reducing me to what seemed like a long, slow crawl through the hallways. Because our hallways were wide enough that I could regain my balance by grabbing onto a wall, taking big steps, or finding the locker of a friend to lean on, I managed to be okay.

Kaela was in college in Boston, and I noticed her FA progressing too, but in different ways. I still walked; she was in a scooter. I've met other FA patients who have developed diabetes, passed away from heart malfunctions, or used a wheelchair their whole life. Some developed late-onset FA (diagnosed after their childhood years); others developed early-onset FA (diagnosed before adulthood). Knowing other people's journeys with FA did not help prepare me for mine. The experiences manifest so differently that I couldn't try to mimic anyone else's path the way I once tried to mimic certain dunks, fade-away jumpers, or batting stances.

Kaela's progression didn't provide clues about my future, but noting how she dealt with FA was extremely helpful. I could undoubtedly mimic her hard-working, self-reliant attitude. Kaela was—and still is—a fighter. She had plans for an education, a career, and an independent life, all of which she's achieved. That determination was something I wanted.

Beginning in high school, I upped my hour-long exercise sessions from once a week to three or four times per week. The school's physical trainer became a close friend and developed a great workout plan customized for me. Even while he trained thirty other athletes, he always helped me one-on-one. "Joey," he would say to me, "every human being has to breathe, drink water, eat, and sleep during a day to function, so you must add exercise into that daily mix and keep your air, food, and drink as clean as possible."

That was logic that never left me, and I knew at a younger age than most how imperative exercise and nutrition are to warding off medical problems. Teenagers don't want to think about how dangerous it is to forget putting orthotic insoles in your shoes or ponder the unhealthy nutritional facts of a large Number Two with a Coke from McDonald's. While the student-athletes focused on shaving a few seconds off their sprints or lowering their BMI, my goals were to be strong enough to walk and stand without assistance, transfer myself into the driver's seat, my bed, and shower, and dress myself without stumbling or falling.

With my balance issues becoming more prevalent, focusing on walking from classroom to classroom caused me to breathe as heavily as an obese man attempting a 400-meter dash. Fatigue and physical stress deeply affected my focus in class and my ability to exercise after school. My brain and body were always exhausted. But I adapted and learned to push past it. To get stronger, I had to get used to being uncomfortable.

The teachers at school who knew about my FA, like Coach Kev, allowed me and a friend to take the elevator, usually forbidden from student use. But whenever the hallways were packed, I wouldn't take it, because I didn't want people to see me. The friend-chaperone was supposed to make me look more casual, like walking with that person was just a social movement, so I would not feel "different." To my surprise, this ended up producing the opposite effect because other kids would stare in jealousy and wonder as I took advantage of the elevator privilege.

I didn't handle the decline in my ability to walk very well—at all. Becoming less and less independent ate me up. I could handle losing my strength and coordination, but not being able to walk from one classroom to the other without assistance frightened me. It caused me to stop doing the things I enjoyed, like going to the beach, going to Fenway Park, or running errands. I still didn't want to talk to anyone about my new challenges, so I swallowed them whole.

But in Coach Kev's class, life was easy. I didn't care about my appearance in that class because I knew my teacher was on my side; there were no secrets between us. I guess you could say Coach Kev was a hero to me. Mark Twain wrote, "We find not much in ourselves to admire; we always privately want to be like somebody else. If everybody was satisfied with himself, there would be no heroes." If I could have been anyone else at the time, it would have been Coach Kev ... except for the part about wearing a sweater vest. (He could rock it, though.)

He was about six feet tall, a young father, and wore a sweater vest over his tie every day like a boss. Because he had three children and his wife was an elementary school teacher, he knew how dumb Snapchat filters were, how smiling in photos was social suicide for teenage boys, and how Tom Brady was known as the "goat emoji" of NFL quarterbacks online.

Knowing students' attention spans were fragile at best, he would put history lessons and characters into the context of our real lives, like comparing JFK and RFK's brotherly power dynamic to Peyton and Eli Manning. Or, comparing Pearl Harbor and the

Bay of Pigs to the Patriots' Super Bowl win over the Panthers and the Patriots' Super Bowl loss to the Giants.

His lessons were not always about U.S. history. For example, he taught us about the ramifications of allowing ourselves to be in a public video and warned us that even though our antics might seem funny now, in eight years, an employer would Google it and decide not to hire us. He cared about us—he didn't want to see us hurt ourselves out of pure stupidity—and that earned him a high score in the hero department.

By the time the spring semester rolled around, we had researched topics of our choice for oral presentations on the most substantial leader from the U.S. during the Cuban Missile Crisis. The presentation would count as a quarter of our final grade.

No pressure.

It was around that same time when incoming new students shadowed classes. It was a school tradition. I had been like them once: scrawny, clueless, and terrified. Coach Kev's class was one of the classes five of the newcomers visited to observe the lessons and the interactions between students and teachers.

The day I was scheduled to present was the day the new students would be there. I was more than prepared. With so much of our final grade at stake, I'd worked extremely hard on my talk about RFK's secret role in the Cuban Missile Crisis. I'd diligently emailed my PowerPoint to Coach Kev that morning.

As you can imagine, I wasn't thrilled about the idea of presenting in front of the class. And now, compounding my usual anxiety about public speaking (or public spitting) was the fact that I'd be doing it in front of a bunch of hormonal eighth-grade shadows.

As I awaited my turn, I mapped out my walk from my chair to the projector and back to my seat. I was sure I would trip over someone's backpack on the floor. I chugged water to keep my tongue moist, so my speech impediment would go unnoticed. Dry mouth is nobody's friend.

"Joey Mullaney," Coach Kev called as he looked down at his class roster. I was up. Suddenly, it didn't matter that I was prepared and had given myself a pep talk. My legs turned off like a powered-down robot.

"Um," I called out, "Coach, I mean, Mr. Wiercinski, I didn't get a chance to finish it."

I didn't know why I was lying since:

1. Coach Kev knew me so well.

2. I had already emailed him my presentation. (He did not see the email, I would later learn.)

3. I knew the information inside and out!

Was this self-preservation, or was I a coward?

The incoming shadows turned to Coach Kev, scrutinizing him for a chink in his armor. I knew this was not a good position to put him in. I'd completely undermined his authority, and whatever his next move was could affect his reputation with next year's incoming students. Either he would be known as a pushover or a strict teacher. Regardless, I had screwed this one up for us both. I expected him to go with me on this, like an improv comedy duo. But he didn't take the approach I had dreamed up.

I'd expected Coach to let FA take the blame and give me a pass. Instead, Coach Kev not only yelled at me for not having my presentation ready, but he lost it on the entire class for having terrible presentations. He was so mad, he told us all to go to lunch even before class ended. "I've seen enough," he said angrily.

Appetite lost. Guilt. Remorse. Regret.

I felt all of it sitting at my desk while the rest of the class ran off to an early lunch. Putting Coach Kev on the spot and taking advantage of our unique relationship might have made him feel trapped. I wasn't sure. I needed him to know the truth about the situation, and I needed to apologize. He was so dismissive. I knew that was not him, not the real Coach Kev. But I hadn't shown him the real Joey either. We had both been untrue to ourselves and to each other. I wanted him to know I knew this. I tried to make it right and do better by both of us.

Once everyone left the room except us two, I looked at Coach as he logged out of his computer. "I swear, Coach, I would never blow off your assignments, ever! You have to know that," I pleaded. Losing the respect of my hero was something I couldn't handle. The thought of letting him down, of him thinking I had let myself down too, cut deep.

"Coach Kev, please check your email, please! Check! I swear it's there! I was ju--, just afraid." I pinched my nose to build a dam for my swelling tears, found my desk, and tried to bury my head into it.

Then, as if a hypnotist had snapped his fingers, Coach Kev stopped what he was doing to look at me. Coach emerged from his enraged trance, remembering my condition and our relationship. "Oh, Joey, I totally blanked out for a second. I am so sorry," he said, his eyes locked on mine. "Joe, I messed up. I believe you sent it. Trust me. I just ... totally forgot about ... I'm so sorry."

I sensed his shame and disgrace. That was my fault. I had made him feel that way, burdened him with my issues. Here I was walking around school, pretending I didn't have FA, and requesting that I get as little special treatment as possible—*except* for when I wanted it, like during oral presentations. What a hypocrite I was! I hated myself for putting Coach Kev on the spot, for making him somehow feel as if he had done something wrong by managing his classroom and upholding his authority. I didn't want him to look at me anymore. My arms encased my face in hopes he couldn't see the tears that ran down my cheeks onto his desk. Coach placed a box of tissues in front of me—an olive branch.

"Stay here as long as you want, Joey. It's safe here," he said. Coach Kev sat at his desk and pretended to scribble some notes. That was the last thing he said to me before I left the room. It felt like my stomach was opening up into my throat, and before I knew it, my moans were echoing against the blue tiles of the handicap-accessible stall in the boys' bathroom. I had locked myself in just like I had locked myself inside my cage of lies and denial. All this wailing caused a lot of junk to come out of me unexpectedly. It was like that moment in *The Green Mile*, when John Coffey projectile-vomits all those nasty bugs in one gut-wrenching spill. I was choosing to swallow too much, and it was coming back up now in ways I didn't want.

Exhausted, I splashed water on my face and tried to resurrect Social Me. But I couldn't think up a good prank to play on my friends, recall a self-deprecating story to tell the girls, or summon the energy to flash the perfect smile to my science teacher.

As I sat alone in the accessible stall debating whether to unlock the door, I realized something. I had depended on others to build me up, keep my secrets, and consider my fears and insecurities. I'd relied on the opinions and actions of others to determine my value. Expecting someone to automatically understand your deeply personal issues is not fair, and it only gets you locked up in a cage of your own creation.

Not only that, I was trying to have it both ways.

I didn't want people to question me or my abilities, but I had the audacity to lean on FA when I wanted to and then expect people to pivot along with me at a moment's notice. I didn't want to be self-centered, but thinking that the world will meet you where you are is pretty much the definition of selfishness. When it came to expectations, I'd put them all on Coach Kev. And as I rallied the inner strength to let myself out of the stall, I decided to focus on what Coach Kev was giving me that day, and every other day, that made him stand out among so many other people in this world. He wasn't offering me heroics; he showed me his humanness.

CHAPTER 17

Like a Virgin

Sex. It's on the mind of every kid in high school. *How does it work? What exactly do I do? Where should I buy condoms? (You know ... so I'm prepared.)* Just like those actors in movies like *Superbad* and *Project X*, teenage boys keep telling themselves The Deed will happen. I was now an upperclassman, and I'd spent most of my adolescent years repeating the mantra to myself: *It will happen. It will happen.* Truthfully, the wondering if and when it would happen was more of an extension of my hyper-awareness over my delay in height. I had finally reached five-ten, but it had taken a few years for me to grow those extra inches. I'd always been behind my friends in that department. I wondered how many years behind my friends I'd be when it came to losing my virginity.

I just assumed my friends all had their first times behind them and were now regularly enjoying this phenomenon with their significant others. My buddies didn't necessarily say they had lost *it* already, but they also didn't say they hadn't. Being vague allowed a certain air of mystery. Real men don't kiss and tell because they don't have to—they've done *it*. So keeping your private life on the DL was a good strategy.

Since everyone had mastered the "I've already done *it*" act by staying silent, I joined in. I didn't want to be looked down upon (or even worse, pitied) by my buddies. Talking about sex never happened. Instead, we talked about circumstances that would lend a hand in the sex and virginity departments—namely, parties.

In one case, I was planning to ask a girl out after getting to know her for about a month. My buddy Marty who told us many stories about his experience involving *it*, gave me advice: "Take her to get ice cream if you want to get serious. Trust me." We all went from speaking English to talking in code from there on out.

"Doug's parents are traveling, so he's thinking about having some friends over," Teddy said in the locker room, rummaging through his gym bag for deodorant. *Poof!* An image appeared in my head, revealing a very hopeful scenario for me. Teddy added, "Ashley told me she's bringing some friends from across town too," which was code for an opportunity to use some corny new pickup lines on them. The best part was the girls didn't already know me!

"You guys want to grab dinner?" Darrien asked, shouting from inside one of the shower stalls. It was only a few weeks before summer vacation, and the boys had just finished their pickup basketball game while I hung around on the sidelines. Friday nights were our regular night to grab food and decompress. Close to campus was a hole-in-the-wall sub shop run by four workers, which meant it was *delicious*. Those guys, brothers, had zero patience for us—six high school boys, obnoxious and loud. They would roll their eyes whenever we came in. But they had great cheap food. You could get two footlong Italian subs for the price of one!

While standing in line debating whether to get the Italian sub deal or only a steak-and-cheese sub before deciding I'd do both, we talked about Doug's party. "I'm pumped for Doug's party tomorrow night!" Teddy said as we sat down with our meals. "Well, not a party, because I heard he's only going to invite a few people over besides us," he added. That was code for a low-key evening, probably with the guy-to-girl ratio being pretty much even.

"And there's a massive Nor'easter coming our way," added Jamie. That was code that it might be too dangerous for us to drive home. "Ashley is going, and she's bringing her hometown friends from a different school. Ashley told me that she always catches her friend, Sloan, stalking Joey's Instagram profile," Teddy said with a mouthful of meatball sub. "Oh, no way, that's awesome!" I replied, slugging down my soda to prevent the guys from seeing me blush with excitement. Rocco shoved me jokingly. "Again?! Damn, Joey, ladies sure do love you! I mean, I don't see it!"

Sitting in the booths of that otherwise vacant restaurant, like we always did, ready to shove heart attacks down our throats, I felt dumb. I mean, these were my best friends. Why should I care if they knew I was still a virgin? Every time I nodded at their stories about going to different house parties without parents, it was just my way of fitting into what I assumed was their brave new world of sex.

"Well," I said, searching for the right words, "about that. I may have led you guys to believe certain things. And when I say *may*, I mean that I *did*. So, you guys know how I said that Christina and I did *it* at her party last spring? That's not true. We just went to her car and made out. So, I'm actually a virgin."

My cheeks turned bright red. The silence was interrupted only by the crinkling of foil sandwich wrappers. And then, Jamie and Mike also confessed simultaneously. "Me, too." "Yeah, me too, bro. It's not a big deal."

"Nobody cares. I mean, *it* is going to happen if you want. Just wait," Teddy said, and the other three guys agreed.

All that overanalyzing for nothing! The reality was, nobody cared. And why would they have been so concerned about *my* virginity, anyway? It would be more in their best interests to focus on their own. Still, the news about Ashley's potentially cute friend who just happened to be into me both freaked me out and encouraged me. I decided I wanted The Deed to be done at the gathering the next night.

Back on FA Night, when I was thirteen, many questions and fears had rattled through my brain. None of them had to do with my "man parts." But as I got older and started noticing weird things happening to my body, I wondered how FA would affect me in that way. Whether *it* would be impacted negatively, like the way FA impacted my speech, balance, and ability to move my legs. I knew FA was paralyzing my body from the toes up, so it did cross my mind to wonder whether other parts of me wouldn't work well. The questions I asked were only to Google, with The Deed potentially happening in the next twenty-four hours.

How will this work? She and I will, I guess, be lying down. Well, I'm not sure …

With whom? A wild guess would be with Ashley's (jaw-dropping) friend.

How do you even know what to do? I don't. But I'm a Millennial with a phone that has the internet on it. I have easy access to figure it out.

Can I have sex, like medically? Well, I think so?

Will FA shut off your "Jimmy John"? I hope not.

If a girl sees me in my boxers, will she take a look at my tiny legs and assume that was a preview of other tiny things about my body? Uh-oh. I'm in trouble.

When I was not fretting about logistics and sex choreography, my mind worried about bigger issues. After all, sex often leads to babies; babies lead to being up all night and changing shitty diapers twenty-five times a day. As terrible as all that sounds to a teenager, one day, as an adult, it might be your greatest wish to have a spouse, kids, and a family—even if that means dark circles under your eyes and smelly garbage cans.

The truth is, that beautiful madness might *not* be in my future. I need help walking, exercising, doing laundry, getting dressed, cooking, cleaning, etc. If I have trouble taking care of myself, how will I take care of my child once FA progresses? How will I hold a baby? How will I change diapers? How will I feed my child? Teach the baby life skills? Protect my family? Nurture the baby? I could just see myself as an adult, dragging my baby to my physical therapy appointments and having my therapist take the baby out of its car seat after helping *me* out first.

The thought of reproducing led me to imagine that the mother of my child—a swimsuit model, obviously—would have to take on more responsibility with our adorable offspring. But, what if she also had to take care of *me*? With her serving as a double nanny, I would be nothing more than a large baby. What kind of spouse wants that?

At this point in my thoughts, I circled back to why any girl would want to do *it* with me in the first place. That whole cycle was exhausting, so I tried to push everything out of my mind and leave my concerns for Future Joey. Today Joey needed to focus on the potentially cute girl who was into me. I reasoned with myself: *I can't worry about manhood until I officially enter it, and hopefully, that will be tomorrow.*

Mother Nature was on my side as she sent steady rain and thunder with a flurry of dense snow that kept Doug's parents from flying home from their vacation. About ten of us showed up at his house—a smart move on Doug's part, since that was a manageable number of kids and we wouldn't destroy his house.

We all brought beer and hung around in his basement, drinking, listening to music, and playing pong. Ashley was there with her friend Sloan. (No, not Sloan from *Entourage*.) She'd just whipped my friends at beer pong, but I pretended not to notice her—a classic move Marty had taught me. About halfway through the party and my twelve-pack, Sloan walked over to my side of the basement.

My liquid courage helped me talk to her instead of looking over at her every thirty seconds, hoping to make eye contact. Sloan was short with brown eyes and a great big smile. At first, our conversation was just small talk: *What college do you want to go to? Have you been to any concerts?* I thought my buddies were going to tease and laugh at me for talking with a girl. Thankfully, this wasn't elementary school anymore, and nobody cared what I was doing.

As the night went on, with constant flirtatious touching, our small talk shifted into real talk: *Are you planning to go away to college? What's your take on God?* That led to, "I think you're really cute, Joey. Do you want to talk in a quieter area, upstairs?"

Her invitation was *the* code, according to movies. "Don't worry. I'll help you walk up. Your brother told me about your situation, and it's all good."

Huge! I never thought I would say this, but thanks, Sean!

Thank goodness I was enjoying the beverages. If not, I probably would have responded obliviously, "No one else is up there, though." Instead, I casually answered, "Yeah, for sure. It's pretty loud down here, anyway."

We went up one flight to the living room where nobody was, sat together on the couch, and started kissing while everyone else was partying downstairs. At about the same time my lips began to burn, she stopped and said, "Do you want to go upstairs to a bedroom?" italicizing "upstairs" *with her hands.* It was like I was in some making-out version of Donkey Kong, slowly leveling up several flights of stairs.

Partly because I don't want this book to turn into an R-rated book, but mostly because my mom will be reading it, all I can do now is pan to the crackling embers of a slow-burning fireplace, call "Scene!" and hope you figure out the rest.

(Spoiler alert: *It* happened.)

Overall, I'd give myself an A for effort and an F for performance. That averages out to a C, so I'll take it.

CHAPTER 18

From Anonymous to Assembly

According to curefa.org, Friedreich's ataxia affects about one in every 50,000 people in the United States. Most individuals experience the onset of symptoms of FA between the ages of five and eighteen years. Adult or late-onset FA is less common, but it can occur any time during adulthood. According to the website, the signs and symptoms of FA are:

- loss of coordination (ataxia) in the arms and legs
- fatigue, energy deprivation, and muscle loss
- vision impairment, hearing loss, and slurred speech
- aggressive scoliosis (curvature of the spine)
- diabetes mellitus (insulin-dependent, in most cases)
- serious heart conditions, including hypertrophic cardiomyopathy and arrhythmias

The site goes on to say, "The mental capabilities of people with Friedreich's ataxia remain completely intact. The progressive loss of coordination and muscle strength leads to motor incapacitation and the full-time use of a wheelchair."

One rainy Sunday, I was enjoying the rare quiet of my house and binge-watching *Entourage*. Like any respectable lazy person, I held my pee until I got hungry. The plan was to make one round trip instead of two: pee and make myself a sandwich, but finish watching TV first. I hadn't moved a muscle for the entire morning, and when I stood up from the couch, I dropped to the floor, my useless legs folding under me.

DAMMIT.

This moment was precisely what all my working out had been about, to be able to lift my dead weight—all 150 pounds of it—but I don't think I ever really believed it would happen. I was not training for a sport anymore but for this and whatever followed. My feet felt hollow. Somehow my bladder took a backburner to my worry.

How long would it take me to stand up and stay up? Was this morning the last time my legs would take me to the couch? Had I just wasted hours of my day lying around when I could've walked for maybe the last time ever? I'm home alone; what if this happens again?

I managed to get myself up. I measured my steadiness for about thirty seconds before moving one foot in front of the other. After another minute, the hollowness filled. *With blood? With oxygen?* I think it was confidence. Like a sports car that sat in a garage during the winter months, my body needed a few turns of the engine to get going again, and I had proven I could come to my own rescue if necessary.

The dormancy of sleep produced a similar result to my couch marathon. I got used to it as I grew a little older. Falling out of bed became my new routine. I tried to plant my feet like my trainer at LA advised, but nope! Faceplant! My brain told my body, "Come on and get up, Joe. You have to take a piss." But FA said, "Yeah, no. You are mine, and you do what I want you to do." When I could feel my muscles retaliate against the numbness, they were in spasms. Visible ripples beneath my skin looked like a snake skimming the surface of a murky river. Over time, those spasms got worse and worse, the snake faster and more pronounced.

I heard someone say once that everyone is suffering. In one way or another, there is a problem, a challenge, an issue, a conundrum, a wrong choice, or a difficulty we are all dealing with. This thought is a grounding reality for me and keeps me from complaining. I try to look at the Oprahs and the Kevin Ogars of the world, people who have faced adversity and overcome it without complaining or asking, "Why me?" Instead, they looked to the stars and changed the question to "Why *not* me?" I try very hard to have that mindset. FA sucks, but even though others might not have my exact issue, they have their own shit.

"Don't complain" became one of my mantras during tough times. But I cannot lie. These physical drains were starting to feel like a tsunami. When I was thirteen, I couldn't see it from a distance, but now, all of these little earthquakes were creating larger and larger waves. FA was stealing my abilities and washing away my life as I knew it. There was nothing I could do to stop the flood.

For many years, Lawrence Academy has hosted a camaraderie event in which the entire student body and faculty climb Mount Monadnock in southeast New Hampshire to kick off each school year. The mountain peaks at over 3,100 feet high and has many hiking trails. LA reserves the entire pathway of a few trails to the top of the mountain for the afternoon. Over 400 students and forty faculty members can hike and be loud and obnoxious without annoying the general public. We were to leave campus via bus at 10 a.m. and travel to the base of the mountain, an hour and a half away.

Before the voyage, we were greeted by motivational speaker Travis Roy in our campus assembly room. Travis told us his story of resilience and triumph over self-doubt and hard luck. Travis had earned a full scholarship to play hockey at Boston University and was projected to play in the NHL one day. Eleven seconds into his first on-ice appearance as a college freshman, Travis went to check the defender, but missed and slammed headfirst into the boards. Doctors discovered that he had cracked a vertebra and was paralyzed from the neck down. All that work, sacrifice, and hope … all those summers he spent (like my athlete friends) at drills, camps, and workouts … it was all for a mere eleven seconds of playing time. Thirty years later, Travis was running his own nonprofit and was a motivational speaker and author who traveled the country inspiring others to take ownership of their lives. When I read his book, *11 Seconds,* I felt like my world could open up. I felt like there was hope.

After listening to Travis and then enjoying a very rambunctious commute to Mount Monadnock, my schoolmates and I unloaded into an empty parking lot surrounded by thirty-foot trees. Our headmaster gave all of the hikers instructions: "Walk in single file on the trails, leave no trash on the ground, no mudslinging, and as always … have fun!" We were to meet back at the campsite for lunch. This day marked the third year in a row I took the bus ride but did not do the hike. Freshman year, I was in a walking boot because I'd sprained my foot. Sophomore year I said my asthma—which had not been prevalent since I was nine—was acting up. This year, after the spills I'd been taking getting out of bed, I knew there was no chance I could get one toe onto the trail without killing myself. So, I said I did not have my inhaler with me, and that was that. We took no chances. Not every faculty member knew my real truth, but the ones who did went along with me. Rocco, who was on the football team, and other in-season athletes also were permitted not to hike so they wouldn't hurt themselves.

During the three-hour wait for the hikers to return for lunch, we played cards, napped, and talked about the Pats. Rocco knew the real reason I sat out, but I wondered if the others ever realized why. Every athlete was recognizable; so were the injured kids. But I looked "healthy," no walking boot or sling or crutch as proof. When the hike was over, starving kids lined up for a lunch buffet. Rocco knew it would be tough for me to stand, wait, and grab food in the buffet line while walking along the rocky, uneven mountain base. He grabbed two plates, and I sat at a table, reserving his seat.

Even without hiking, I was physically spent just from walking around the base on the harsh landscape, trying to be an energetic, friendly kid. Even though I sat around most of the day, those few hours had made me weak. The weaker I became, the more tired I looked, and the worse my balance and coordination got. An hour-long nap on the bus back to school did not help at all. Back on campus, I was determined to be Social Me and join the hundreds of kids in the student lounge before going home, sharing pics and telling stories that happened on the hike.

The student lounge was a large hangout spot full of lockers, couches, work tables, and vending machines. The freshmen and sophomores hung around the lockers and couches; the juniors and seniors hung around the tables and vending machines. I immediately went to sit down at one of the tables with many other kids. Then Toni, whom I knew well-ish but who didn't know about FA, ran up to me with a concerned look. "Joey, what's wrong? Your walking is off. Are you okay?" she asked, squeezing my arm.

I'd heard people describe themselves as a deer in headlights, but today the metaphor was my own. I was the deer. I'm actually very good at handling awkward situations. But the concern in Toni's voice mixed with her worried, confused look left me at a loss for words. Just like the day I had to use my upper-body strength to pick myself off the floor, I never really thought this day would come, when my weakness would be so obvious, a friend would bluntly show concern. I wasn't mad, but my house of cards had just fallen, and I didn't have the strength to pick them up. So, I copped out. I pulled the old "throw the burden on your close friend" trick.

"Uh, yeah, I don't know," I muttered as I began to hyperventilate and sweat. I looked around the room and saw Jennifer. I had known Jen well since we were in many classes together and we ended up becoming very close friends. I never told Jen about my not-so-secretive disease, but somehow she knew.

Toni kept standing there, waiting patiently for my response. *I wish she'd let go of my arm.*

"Just go ask Jen, please," I said, twiddling a straw wrapper. "She'll tell you."

Toni took my cue.

"Okay, Joey," she said and walked over to the group of girls laughing and flashing their phones to one other.

I felt alone and wanted very much to be alone, so I stumbled out of the lounge to my car, where I could think. I lowered my driver's seat so it was horizontal, to make sure nobody walking by could see me through the window.

This war with FA had gone rogue on me. I had nothing in me anymore, no fight, just the reality that on a beautiful, bright, sunny September day, I felt a hundred years old. I couldn't pretend any longer. If Toni could see it, others definitely could too.

It did not dawn on me that I had put Jennifer in an impossible position. She had been loyal to me by not sharing my secret for years. Now she was being ambushed by Toni. *How could Jen be sure I wanted my business shared? What did she even say to Toni? Did she feel like she was caught in a predicament?*

This is not how I ever wanted to operate. I'd never planned to avoid my responsibility to deal with my issues, nor to send a friend off to discuss business that is only mine to discuss. Maybe saying it out loud would make it too real? *It was real*, but only in my world full of close loved ones. I relished the fake world where I was a normal kid. Now, that artificial world was fading like a memory.

I was stunned in multiple ways, just completely caught off guard. If a girl I was barely friends with was willing to say something, who would be next? *The hottest senior girl during lunch with 400 students and faculty?* Up to this point, even if people had noticed, they either stared or walked away, but they never confronted me. Toni asked me because she cared and was concerned for me, so I couldn't be mad. But it meant I couldn't hide my problem anymore.

On the drive home, I told Sean what had happened. He gave me a stunned look of his own. He could see my red cheeks and how out of breath I was. He was shocked that people noticed or knew, and he didn't like not knowing who those people were. Without my knowing, he told my parents later that night about the incident.

The next day, Sean and I got an email saying to meet with the Dean of Students, Mrs. Margraf, and my advisor, Mr. Culley, during lunchtime. Mr. Culley, who knew me, Sean, my parents, and my situation well, was a six-foot-two, 210-pound muscular dude who served as a firefighter on the weekends. When the walkways were icy during the winters, Mr. Culley would text me before I got to school to warn me. One morning, he saw me entering school with a big gash over my eyebrow. I had fallen getting out of the shower that morning and hit my head on the bathroom countertop. He took one look at me, ripped off the bandage, and saw that the cut was still bleeding—almost an hour after I'd fallen. After LA's weekly student body and faculty assembly, he drove me to the ER to get stitches.

This time, we went into Mrs. Margraf's office. Her oversized mahogany desk made a statement of authority, sturdiness, and importance. She sat behind her desk, Sean and I sat on the two chairs in front of the desk, and Mr. Culley pulled up a chair next to us.

Mrs. Margraf began: "I do not want to waste anyone's time, so let's get right to it. Joey, Sean and your parents made us aware of the situation yesterday after we all got back from the mountain." I gave Sean a death look while he responded with an innocent shrug and said, "Joe, I had to. Mom and Dad should know." I ignored him to talk to Mrs. Margraf.

"Please do not get Toni in trouble. She did nothing wrong!" I said.

"We know, Joey. That's not why you're here," Mrs. Margraf said with her most rational tone. "She did nothing wrong. But this terrible situation can't keep happening—for you and your family's sake. We all can prevent this situation from snowballing into something worse soon if we strategize and take the right approach."

This was the Lawrence Academy way, to invite everyone to take a singular approach to figure out a complex problem, together. Except Mr. Culley threw a curveball.

"Joey, this has gone beyond some busybody students. I've been approached by many concerned teachers and staff, asking why you walk as if you're intoxicated and if you are okay." He leaned forward intently, gripping his fist with his hand, to make his next point. "You must understand that I, Mrs. Margraf, and Coach Kev cannot keep lying to our colleagues any longer, Joe."

"We think your peers can help," Mrs. Margraf said. Her voice stern and steady, she made the answer sound definitive, as if she'd polled the student body or something. "We all just have to tell them. ASAP."

And by "we," she meant ME as she pitched her strategic plan for me to go on stage in front of the whole SCHOOL during our weekly ASSEMBLY, and give a SPEECH about my life-sucking DISEASE.

School, assembly, speech, disease. I need to get out of here!

"No way—not happening," I snapped. I wanted to run out, but as you know, that was not an option. Innocent Mr. Culley fell silent. He mustered up the strength to plead with me, because he cared.

"Joey," he said, still gripping his hands but now pressing them together like he was about to say a prayer, "there comes a time for everyone where limits end. The attempt for normalcy is doing the opposite for you. You are using too much of your mental space. I think you're acting a little off from your usual self. I'm afraid you might find it harder to get through schoolwork and focus on getting into college. It's like you're wearing a ton of bricks on your back, and you can't go far with that kind of weight on you, and we want to see you go far. We know you can if you can unburden yourself."

Well said, Mr. Culley. Wait a second ... Is this the part of the movie where the mentor gives the big pep talk and I'm supposed to buy in? Cue the comeback music.

I laughed and then said, "Am I being punked?! Where's Ashton?"

"Joey, come on. This isn't a joke," Sean said, breaking his silence. "You can explain FA, the simpler parts. You can ask for help. Tell them how people can help. Holding doors open, moving out of the way in the hallways and cafeteria, locking arms with you when walking, helping you carry heavy textbooks."

Wait ... That all sounded pretty good. And I knew the stuff about narratives was right. If I didn't control it now within LA, people would just make up their judgments of me, and they would 100 percent of the time be wrong. But to tell the whole school? I didn't see how I could ever do it.

I thought about everything for thirty seconds and then said, "Okay, I'm listening."

Mrs. Margraf had already drafted some of what she would say at the assembly. She cleared her throat and read from her notepad, "Many of you have shown concern for your classmate, Joey Mullaney. It is no secret he has not been himself, and it is refreshing to see the community show such concern and worry." After a few more comments, she would turn it over to Mr. Culley to explain FA's details and what it means to have it—all the clinical stuff, just the facts. Then, he would introduce me so I could share my story and explain how everyone could help. That's where they lost me.

"Wait. I'm sorry, everyone, but I can't get up there. I don't feel comfortable speaking," I said, unwavering. Then I added emphatically, "Staring at everyone while they're staring at me, pitying me because my life is a ticking timebomb ... I'm not going."

Silence filled the room, somehow making it feel empty. Nobody knew how to respond. And then, Sean raised his voice and asked, "What if I did it?"

The thought of exposing my medical history and issues to the entire school, details that affect me daily, was utterly cringe-worthy. I waited in Mrs. Margraf's office while the student body filed into the auditorium, as it did every Tuesday morning. Sean was sitting on a folding chair on stage. He was taking the heat while I hid away. I knew somehow, though, this would be the most challenging part. It was time. I could not outrun my reality anymore.

Walking to class after it was over, I received four text messages, each from a different girl telling me she loved me. When I walked into my Spanish class after the other sixteen students were already seated, my classmates were quiet as they moved their backpacks from the aisle so I could get through. Doors were opened, and elevators were no longer used without a legit reason. And my friends still called me a tool. I was happy. The tidal wave had crashed over, and I was still alive. I hadn't been drowned by the truth.

What I learned that day all comes down to acceptance. You can't stop something out of your control, so accepting it is the key to surviving it. When you accept something, you can work with it, make it work for you, even defend and prepare yourself better for life after it. Staring at a monstrous storm with deer-in-the-headlights eyes and a gaping mouth while crapping yourself is not going to help you survive. With the help of trusted people, it was time to look at the frightening wave with a smile and decide what to do after it passed. For this wave, Sean threw me a life preserver. He defended me from the unknown.

Actually, Sean didn't just throw me a life preserver—he *was* my life preserver. Telling the community of Lawrence Academy about FA had enabled me to stop hiding from myself. I felt like the old me again, unafraid to be seen in public; my personality and sense of humor were no longer cowering in the darkness. I had not given people the benefit of the doubt; I thought they would judge me, laugh at me, or my biggest fear, feel sorry for me. Instead, they gave me the courage to begin offering the world the real me.

CHAPTER 19

Dunk City

After the outpouring of support and love from my peers at Lawrence Academy, it was like a switch had been flipped back on. At first, I was a bit mad at myself for wasting so much time being afraid. But I knew the right thing to do was to chalk it up to a good learning experience, from which I had gained the wisdom of my new truth. I carry this overall experience with me to this day. It taught me that the time I have left in this world is my friend, not my enemy.

I felt like I was finally back in the game. As luck would have it, I had some tremendous opportunities presented to test my newfound mojo. When our peers asked Sean and me to go on stage at the next assembly to perform a skit celebrating National Twin Day, I said yes. The next fall, when asked to be the first Senior Speaker to deliver a speech to the entire community, I said yes. When asked to become a senior peer leader to help first-year students through their orientation, I said yes. When asked to accept the senior superlative of "Best Personality," I said yes.

I did not hesitate to sit in the middle of the bleachers at crowded sporting events if those were the only available seats, even though getting through a sea of legs was nearly impossible for me.

I was done losing my shit because I was afraid of giving a presentation in front of the class. Gone were the days of making up excuses, or worse—Sean doing it for me. Never again would he have to lie about why I wasn't on the basketball team with him.

It might be cliché to say the truth sets you free, but I'm proud to say I know firsthand that that's true. I'm a walking (not so well), talking (and maybe not doing that so well either) example with a pep in my step!

Even though FA did not go away, I did not care. If I needed to lock arms with someone to help me walk without falling, I would. I began to look forward to it, wondering what new peer I was going to ask next. I slept better; I stressed less. And even though Sean and I were always super tight, his addressing the elephant in Mrs. Margraf's office the way he had actually strengthened our bond even more.

When basketball season rolled around, Sean and I intended to make the most of our final season together. Sean would be on the court, and I would be on the bench, keeping the in-game statistics. After three years, our twelve-man team was a pack of best friends. We hung around together at school, went to practice together, and partied on the weekends together. It's safe to say we spent more time with one another than with our families.

In just a few months, heading to college meant I would never sit on the sidelines with a basketball team again (unless the Boston Celtics were interested). Each game, I dressed as a coach in dress pants and a button-down shirt, recording stats to show Coach Kev. The league we played in had teams with legit Division I talent on their rosters. We got to play against New England power-houses like Northfield Mount Hermon, the Tilton School, and the St. Andrew's School. A few of their players, now household names in the NBA, went on to play for elite NCAA programs like Michigan, Kentucky, Kansas, Syracuse, and more.

Our team, on the other hand ... not so much. Our record was less than stellar. But even when we were down thirty or forty points, Coach Kev would not allow anyone to give up and stop playing.

Senior Day was just around the corner, so LA planned a pregame ceremony. Coach Kev would give a speech and each senior would be honored with his parents. Sean and I really anticipated this game.

Earlier in the week, Coach Kev had tracked me down in the hallway between classes. He asked me to come to his office because he needed my help during my free period. He never said what it was. I'm not going to lie—for some odd reason, I felt nervous. *Was I in trouble?* Okay, maybe I'd crossed the line last week when I dressed up like him and mimicked his antics in the locker room after a game, to make my teammates laugh. Even knowing his usual laidback demeanor, my stomach did a flip-flop the way it had when Aunt Statie told me to go with her outside at that Sweet Sixteen party.

What did Coach want?

What had I done? It was a joke, and he laughed … I think.

Was I fired? No. What? I didn't work for him anyway. That would be ridiculous.

Had someone made a complaint about me?

Am I failing his class now?

Will I be able to graduate on time?

I tried to think more positively. Maybe Coach Kev wanted my help to surprise Sean with something on Senior Day. *Yeah, that's it.*

Coach Kev shared a large office with four other history teachers. As I opened the door, I made my way in as I usually did. "What's up, Coach?" I sat in my usual spot, and it made me a little sad to think I would no longer be joking around with him in his office. For now, onto planning Sean's surprise.

"Joey, we all love you. You know that, right?" Coach Kev said, leaning over his desk.

Holy crap. This sounds like a breakup. "It's not you; it's me." Could this be happening?

"Yeaahhh. Love you all too," I said with some hesitation.

"Well, you know Senior Day is coming, and we always do something for the seniors on the team, make a big statement, you know?"

"Yeah," I said, swallowing the lump in my throat. "Planning something for Sean? I know he is not a fan of attention. I recommend making Sean's speech short and sweet. That would be cool."

"Well, okay, but that's not why you're here," Coach said, now with a massive grin on his face. "We know you would do anything to play. I've been with you for four years now and know you deserve the best. So, the other coaches and I were thinking, in the next game, you suit up and score a basket." Coach Kev informed me that the opposing team and the league referees all agreed I would have a *Rudy* moment on Senior Day.

"Whaddya say, Joe? Suit up, do a layup, the crowd goes wild? Show us all you still got it?"

"With all due respect, Coach. Not. Gonna. Happen. Big fat NO. I am not okay with that."

Then Coach Kev gave me one of his legendary pep talks.

"We all need this," he said. "You have a chance to make others happy. Only you can do that. Neither team is making the playoffs anyway. You could score by just a layup, something easy. Your boys will help you, so what do you say?"

Wow, he really wanted me to do this. He was so invested in me. Later, I would realize what a moving gesture this was, but in that moment, I just saw it as a setup for catastrophe. My sports career had ended in eighth grade. I could not play again. I was finally in a good place in my social life where I didn't bring attention to myself, but I didn't need to go to lengths to divert it either. *Why would I do a crazy thing like this? Why was Coach Kev so motivated to talk me into this?*

After I said no a few more times, I left to go to my next class. But whatever was going on in English could not be absorbed. I wasn't in the mood to discuss the reasoning behind the metaphor of the flashing green light in *The Great Gatsby*. Sorry, Ms. Martin. My brain was consumed with thoughts about what Coach Kev had offered. Even though it had only been a few minutes, I already felt a tremendous amount of regret, like when I dumped my fourth-grade girlfriend during recess and she cried in front of everyone and I felt like a terrible person. *I mean, being ten years old and balancing playing manhunt with my neighbors, plus Little League baseball and a girlfriend is stressful. Cut me some slack!*

Once I stopped to think about it, I couldn't believe I'd said no to Coach. I loved the game. My best friends were willing to help. Instead of sitting on the bench, when I always wanted to suit up and run out on the court, I could play. If I turned down the opportunity, what was I telling myself? When opportunities knock, am I just the guy who bolts the door shut?

From class, I texted Coach Kev with two words: "I'm in."

I told him there was one catch, though. I'd only do it on a few conditions.

"Awesome, Joe! Sure! No problem. Let's talk," he texted back.

During lunch that day, Coach Kev came to the student lounge where some guys from the team and I were hanging out. They knew, by now, I was aware of the Senior Day idea.

Coach Kev said, "All right, Joe, what are your conditions?"

"Well, if I'm doing this, I'm doing it big. So, I don't want to score on a layup. I want to dunk."

Coach Kev laughed at my bravado, but I was serious, and my teammates and I had it all figured out. "Coach, I only weigh like 150 pounds. Daquan is six-eight, 215. Daquan texted me saying he's cool with it. I've legit seen him squat 225 pounds. If I'm on his shoulders, I can dunk it. It would be epic!"

Coach Kev said he thought it could happen, but he'd need time to think about how it would all go down. He would get back to us. As he left, Sean stopped him and said he wasn't surprised by my request. "That's just Joey. He has to go out with a bang," he told Coach Kev, who laughed and then responded, "Whatever I come up with, I'll make sure you get the assist to Joe."

Coach Kev worked on a plan to get me back on the court. He drew up the play, and it was the only play we ran later that day for the entire duration of practice. The play:

1. Darrien Myers, the shooting guard, wins the tipoff (the opposing team had agreed) and tips the ball to small forward Jalen Myrie.
2. Center Daquan Sampson and point guard Sean are with me under the basket, holding me up.
3. Jalen passes the ball to Sean while I climb on Daquan's shoulders with Darrien and Jalen's help.
4. To get the assist, Sean passes the ball up to me where I am practically in the sky for the dunk, while Darrien and Jalen hold me up so I don't fall off Daquan's shoulders.

In that practice before the big game between two teams going nowhere, the play worked every time. It was the first time in four years that I was in the team huddle. On this day, during this once-in-a-lifetime practice, *I* was the one who got to break the huddle by yelling, "1-2-3 FAMILY!"

After practice, it seemed as if time were moving in slow motion. I had a distraction: looking for a pair of basketball shoes. Sean and Rocco took me to Foot Locker in the mall to get a pair. I got the brand-new red, white and blue CP3s that matched our school's jerseys, and I felt ready to go. To honor the shoes, I didn't open the box until warmups.

I slept with a full smile across my face. Sean and I got to school early that Saturday morning for the 1 p.m. start. We listened to Drake on the whole thirty-minute drive, just like our old St. Anna days. Our teammate Chris, who was injured, let me wear his uniform for the game, and more importantly, he lent me his Superman socks for good luck. With thirty minutes before tipoff, the team met in the locker room to discuss the play one last time.

I asked each of the team members, the other managers, and the coaches to autograph my new shoes. Holding back tears, I told them it had taken me a lot to get here and that they all played an instrumental part. So that all my teammates could be on the court with me, I had them permanently mark their names on my shoes.

As they formed a circle around me and passed around the black Sharpie, it felt like a tribal council meeting—bonding like blood brothers with a smelly magic marker.

As both teams ran on the court to warm up, I got a glimpse of the packed gym. Before I entered, I had to go to the bathroom. Holding back my breakfast, I splashed water on my face and stared into the mirror, reminding myself, "You can do this. You are ready." Then I made my way to the court.

The Senior Day ceremony took place before the game. The seniors were introduced on the court, accompanied by our parents. Coach Kev had the mic and acted as the enthusiastic emcee, announcing Sean and me last. As he fought back tears,

Coach's speech focused on telling us how sad he was to see us go after four years of being part of the LA family. Then he said something I'll never forget: "Joe, you always thank us for helping you, but we should be thanking you for teaching us to always welcome, then fight through, adversity."

The crowd of people, including parents and rival fans, clapped politely and graciously. During our final pregame huddle, Coach Kev put both of his hands on my shoulders and looked serious. "Joe," he said, "it's the last time I can ask if you want to back out. Do you want to?"

"Fuck that, Coach." And with that, we all laughed.

1-2-3 FAMILY!

The crowd, my mother, and Kaela were confused as to why I was out on the court. Sean and I had divulged the play only to my dad and Ryan, so when they saw me just sitting down at center court, both Mom and Kaela were worried.

The play went off without a hitch, except this time, I could feel the crowd beginning to realize in real time what was happening. As their anticipation floated to the top of the gymnasium, my adrenaline pumped hard. I fed off the room's energy as people began to figure out what I was about to do—and what the other team so graciously let us do. But I did not just put the ball into the basket. I conjured the old Joey, the sixth-grade twerp with the lacrosse stick, who feistily antagonized bigger opponents and got away with it.

I *slammed* that ball into the hoop. It was Dunk City!

FA was my new opponent, and with my teammates' help, I would send a big message to this damned disease once and for all: YOU DO NOT CONTROL ME!

CHAPTER 20

Setting Sail for College

Pivotal moments. If a moment is defined as "a precise point in time," then a pivotal moment must be a specific experience that substantially changes you in some way. Pivotal moments aren't always positive, like back on FA Night when I was told I had this terrible disease. That moment certainly changed me—my outlook, my life trajectory, my goals. Dunk City was no doubt pivotal too. It gave me the tools to transform myself: trust in others, faith in myself, courage to give things a try.

Dunk City never left me. It's still inside me, enabling me to test the waters, push my limits, and see what's out there to conquer. Weeks after Dunk City would come yet another pivotal moment in my life: the decision to participate in our school's annual "Winterim" program.

Every March, this two-week mini-term gave students the chance to break free from the school's routine and go on an experiential learning trip. All students had to participate, and the trip options for seniors were always the most exciting. I don't remember all the possibilities, because as soon as I heard there would be a trip sailing around the Caribbean on a catamaran, I wanted in. We would learn the inner workings of sailing by living on the catamaran, day in and day out, for fourteen days and thirteen nights.

The catamaran I would sail on was over 110 feet long and could fit about sixteen passengers. That sounded like the yachting lifestyle, based on movies I'd seen. I begged my parents to let me go.

To put the trip into perspective, the distance between home plate and first base is ninety feet. So, in essence, sixteen people would sit along the path between home and first at Fenway Park while eating, sleeping, and performing other biological functions for two straight weeks.

Couple that with the fact that the other eleven kids and I would be doing all of our "business" in close quarters with teacher-chaperones, who also would be doing their business. This is what my parents tried to tell me to persuade me to pursue the art history trip twenty minutes away from campus instead.

Living in close quarters didn't worry me despite the challenges I knew I might have getting around the boat. I did, though, worry about being trapped on a boat with a bunch of people I didn't really know. Lawrence Academy was a small school, so we all knew *of* each other. (In the grownup world, this is called "being acquaintances.") But for Teenaged Me, all I could think was, *Oh, shit! I'm going to be stuck with a bunch of strangers!* That said, I figured knowing the faces of my fellow first mates was a luxury, considering that in a few months I was about to venture into completely unchartered territory in college.

In addition to getting used to meeting new people, here is what I discovered while living on a boat:

- The ocean is used as both a toilet and a shower.
- Toilet paper, soap, and shampoo should never be taken for granted.
- The ocean teaches you things about yourself, mainly that you're often powerless against the sea.
- Caribbean March nights are freezing, though the days are melting hot.
- You must rub in sunscreen, not just apply it, to avoid awkward tan lines.

- Sedentary objects are nice.
- Deodorant is a NECESSITY.

Looking back now, I see that I had invited the challenge of living on a boat into my life as some sort of boot camp for what was coming. I would soon be navigating a campus that would be as unsettling as a catamaran cabin on high seas.

Environment is everything, especially when you have FA, and this fact was not lost on my family or me as we began to consider which college campus would meet my needs. The college hunt is all about the right fit.

Picking the right college first comes down to assessing who you are and what you want. Are you a jock from a small, rural town, or a school-oriented student aspiring to graduate with honors? Maybe you are an art-focused student who craves an urban area filled with like-minded artists to network with. Perhaps you're a diehard Southeastern Conference football fan who wants to wake up to the sudden bursts of tubas on gameday. Do you want to be seen and heard in a small classroom environment or hide in the back of a large lecture hall nursing a hangover? Are you looking to study with top scholars, or do you prioritize the guy-girl ratio?

For me, I could only consider these "right fit" questions as a small part of my college hunt. I knew what I wanted, and I knew I needed certain things—and needs come before wants 100 percent of the time.

I needed to dorm away from home; I wanted to become independent and known as Joey, not Sean's twin. I also needed to stay in relative proximity to doctors and family in Massachusetts. So, my range was in New England. North Carolina State was out of the equation.

Of course, I needed a school that was an academic match, but the campus also had to be accessible to a motorized scooter. I knew my stumbling days needed to stop, so I agreed to start using a three-wheeled machine once I was away at school. Almost every school I toured had a significant flaw in the living area, poor accessibility to buildings, or an uneven walkway to class. I was on a quest to find safety, kind of like Sandra Bullock in *Bird Box* (though without blindfolds).

My parents and I had to conduct our own type of campus tours. *Were the roads paved, and were they going to be plowed in the winters?* We tested doors. *Did they feature one of those handy-dandy buttons to automatically open them?* We scoped out the sidewalks. *Were they uneven or even cracked to the point I could have a significant spill and find myself in the middle of campus on my ass with my scooter hovering over me? Were the dormitories handicap-accessible?* My dad's twenty-five-year construction background helped solved the physical problems, while my mom's experience helping Kaela navigate college before me allowed her to provide me with a sense of normalcy during this tough transition.

I wanted to love touring colleges, but it wasn't as much fun as I'd imagined. While other kids were testing out the quality of cafeterias, financial aid packages, libraries, and classrooms, I had to count how many ramps there were or whether my scooter battery could hold a charge from one side of the campus to the other. (Bye bye, UMass!)

Even though I knew that the UConn campus was big enough to warrant its own zip code, I wanted to tour anyway. I wanted to attend a "large–ish" college. It seemed fitting for a sports kid from a sports family like me. Mom was off touring schools with Sean, while Dad drove me to Connecticut. On the day we visited UConn, we got lost going from a classroom to the dorm where I would live and couldn't remember where we'd parked. After thirty minutes of searching, we found our car and crossed that school off my list.

My college search was 180 degrees different from Sean's. Sean was a phenomenal baseball player and was recruited by many schools. So, his criteria were a whole different ballgame. (Pun-ny!)

The next campus visit was at Fairfield University in Connecticut, about an hour and a half from UConn. On the way, we made a pit stop in Wallingford to get gas, and I saw a sign that read:

QUINNIPIAC UNIVERSITY

5 MILES SOUTH

I had heard of that school from watching ESPN; their hockey team was one of the best in the country. While my dad was pumping gas, I sat in the passenger seat and Googled Quinnipiac University (QU) on my phone and saw some beautiful images of the campus. I didn't know if I could get in based on my academics, but why not check it out? My dad was all for it. We went to the campus and were amazed by the modern-day buildings. We couldn't stay long enough to tour more since we had to get to Fairfield before it got dark, but we knew we had to come back.

Upon eventually returning to Quinnipiac, I realized that QU fit me like a glove. It checked all the boxes—every need I had, logistical and otherwise, plus a few wants, which was nice. The dorms and buildings were state-of-the-art, with a few old, Gothic-looking sections. Campus was airy and open with a massive quad, easy to navigate. The sidewalks and roads were well-paved. It was a big campus but not too big. And QU had a great hockey team and other sports programs, which meant parties and tailgates.

I applied early-decision and got in, which was great. This freed up the entire second half of my senior year. From that point forward, I was never preoccupied with doing super-well on essays or exams, nor did I care about another SAT prep course. All I had to do was maintain my 3.4 grade-point average, not get in trouble, and enjoy the rest of my time being a big fish in a little pond. Easy-peasy.

But how would I do in college? What would it be like on my own, vulnerable and alone? Somehow, living on a boat for two weeks gave me a taste of that.

The experiential-learning trip on the catamaran began after we all flew down to St. Maarten from Boston. We would learn all about the intricacies of sailing as we whipped around the islands of the Caribbean. Two teachers chaperoned us. We were led by a captain, a first mate, and a sailing instructor, all employed by the boat charter company. I packed light, as they advised. The day before our plane left, Sean and my parents tried persuading me not to go because they were scared for me. It was the first time I would be without them on a trip, and they were not able to prevent anything from happening to me as they always had on family vacations.

To and from the airport, I planned to use a wheelchair. It would be the first time I would use one since our family vacation to Aruba a few years earlier, and I hated the idea. But after the big assembly and Dunk City, it was common knowledge to everyone within the LA community that I needed help walking.

The entire group was eager to help, and they took turns pushing me. We discovered that wheelchairs and the numerous unpaved roads throughout the Caribbean do not mix well. Many of the locals looked at me like I was an alien, but I didn't mind. Once we got to the catamaran, Captain Mark brought us to the lower deck, where there were two tiny cabins, each with three bunk-beds. We were immediately terrified that we would be stacked like sardines when sleeping. But Captain Mark said that because it always got way too hot down there, we could store our luggage in the cabins and sleep outside on deck.

Sleeping outside in sleeping bags next to one another felt odd at first. But looking out at the mountains, the beautiful water, and the stars made this new experience worth it. Going to the bathroom in close quarters and walking around the boat during the sails was not always fun, but it was doable. Catamarans have many sturdy metal poles to grab onto, so I looked like a monkey swinging around trees as I moved from place to place. All of us cooked, cleaned, made new friends, stepped out of our comfort zones, and learned.

Learning how to ask my peers to help me do things was difficult but became more comfortable. I started with what I knew. Well, with *whom* I knew. My close friend was on the trip too, so it was a little easier to ask him to fetch something below deck or grab me a sandwich while he was getting his own. I graduated to asking the faculty chaperones for help getting around. They were easy to break in because they broke me in first. I don't know what it was about my body language or facial expression, but they both knew before I got the words out of my mouth that I might need something. One of them would often ask me, "Need anything, Joe, while I'm up?" They say necessity breeds ingenuity. In my case, necessity bred humility, and I liked it.

When I wanted to remain stoic and prideful, I saw my fellow mates holding on for balance and thought, *Why shouldn't I do the same?* My peers wheeled me through the airport and down the streets of Caribbean towns, taking turns every fifteen minutes to push me. Each night, two people would pair up to cook dinner for the rest of the students, faculty, and crew. On the night that my close friend and I were the crew's top chefs, we had a few volunteer sous chefs who helped cut vegetables, marinate chicken, and keep the kitchen clean and clear to move around in. During rocky sails, helping hands were everywhere. My stronger mates would throw me on their backs to get me around without risk of me toppling overboard. We began as acquaintances but ended the trip as friends.

I'd never really learned the art of asking for help, because my family had always dutifully been there. I had taken for granted the preemptive things they know to do. I would not have been able to get through the catamaran trip if I hadn't swallowed my pride. And I think I would've alienated and confused people, as well. Instead, we all wound up helping one another. I needed to learn it's okay to be a "taker" sometimes, and my new friends knew to give. That lesson alone would make for smooth sailing for us all as we entered our university years.

CHAPTER 21

Speech!

I try never to show weakness. *Never make your problem some-body else's problem* was a fundamental guiding principle I kept with me growing up. Put mind over matter, deal with issues on your own, work through the pain, and find a way to get past them. These are most definitely the teachings of a sports family. The play-through-the-pain philosophy made me who I am today and certainly primed me to succeed in life despite FA. But, having this mindset is not always easy.

When you're a kid, bottling up your fears and not asking for help is not always wise. I will forever remember my high school experience as the four years that taught me that sucking it up was not the best way to handle my problems. When I finally let others in, I not only made my life much more bearable, I made good friends, got to know myself and my limits much better, and learned about new people.

Being honest about my life became almost like a public service instead of the death sentence I thought it would be. I had made a 180-degree turn from the kid who cried staring out at his cousins in the pool, who almost ruined a relationship with Coach Kev to avoid a presentation, and who stopped going to malls or football games in a quest to avoid telling people my truth. Now, I wanted to speak up in front of people in a formal way. I started to see myself as being responsible for sharing my story because others out there like me, who have it way worse off, might like to hear something hopeful.

Watching inspirational speakers on YouTube became a hobby of mine. I practically memorized Randy Pausch's "The Last Lecture" at Carnegie Mellon University. He was diagnosed with pancreatic cancer and would lose his life at forty-seven years old, less than a year after giving his famous talk. "The brick walls are there for a reason," he said. "The brick walls are not there to keep us out. The brick walls are there to give us a chance to show how badly we want something." Randy gave me a new perspective on my life, and I wished I could deliver something so poignant, something to change a person's mind the way Randy had changed mine. At thirteen years old, I thought FA was my brick wall. Now, I saw a chance to turn FA into a superpower. I had to explore these new gifts. I couldn't stay inside; those days were over. It would be like having the ability to win like Tom Brady or shoot like Kobe Bryant, but choosing to watch TV all day.

It just so happened that my senior seminar class required a six-week project about a topic of my choosing. I saw this as a wonderful time to learn more about speech writing and presenting. This assignment was not typical homework. It demanded dedication to learning and understanding the art and form of public speaking. I had to learn the process of writing, memorizing, rehearsing, and delivering speeches, and it panicked me and fascinated me at the same time. My teacher, Mrs. Moore, served as the advisor for the class. An older woman with white hair and glasses, Mrs. Moore would ask convoluted questions that left us students clueless but forced us to learn more about our topic.

"Are there any guidelines when giving a speech?" Mrs. Moore asked me. "Do you know who Alan Monroe is, and could his five-step motivated sequence benefit your understanding of giving a speech?"

"Ummmm ... yeahhh ... he's the guy with the face. Those five steps will help, probably ... I think so. Most likely? I'll look him up."

Okay, Google Alan Monroe.

Mrs. Moore challenged me because she wanted me to think outside of my comfort zone.

It was ironic that by the time I caught the public speaking bug, FA had affected my physical speech. I was becoming harder to understand as my motor skills deteriorated. I slurred more than ever, breathed more heavily, and salivated more often. Still, Mrs. Moore pressed me. "Use more hand gestures. Make stronger eye contact. Take air from your diaphragm. Shoulders back, chin up, know when to smile and not smile, pause, make a joke, don't joke, enunciate, choose fewer words, choose fewer syllables, inflect your voice, don't spit." She was like a batting coach preparing her team for the big game. It was mind-blowing how challenging it can be to speak to many people, and it became my sport.

Besides researching my topic, which focused on dreaming while living with a physical disability, I had to research the mechanics of giving a speech. One major component is to speak from the heart and stay calm. I could not guarantee the calm part, but Mrs. Moore told me I had the heart for sure. I worried mostly about how I'd be perceived. How would I explain what I wanted to say without getting people depressed or making them think I was looking for attention or pity? I thought about how the pre-assembly Joey would have been too afraid to do it. Then I thought about how Dunk City Joey was afraid but faced his fear and did it anyway.

With graduation only two months away, my 100 graduating class members would pick one girl and one boy to speak at graduation. LA didn't choose a valedictorian. The speakers selected didn't have to be the smartest kids or the most athletic; they just had to win the most votes. A few hours after the votes were tallied, Mrs. Moore saw me in the hallway and bopped over to me with excitement and a giant smile.

"Forget the assigned in-class speech, my friend," she said. "We have to get *you*, Mr. Mullaney, ready to present to about 2,000 grandparents, parents, cousins, friends, students, and loved ones in four weeks. It was just announced. Your peers selected *you* to be a commencement day speaker! I am so thrilled for you!" Then she floated off on an English teacher cloud nine. *I pooped my pants a little.*

After a day of processing that my class had decided I was the last male peer they wanted to hear from before they started the next phase of their lives, I began to feel like an imposter. My classmates didn't know that I was not always positive, that I had been playing hours of video games, listening to Randy Pausch's speeches, and watching NBA highlight videos online to keep from being depressed on certain days. Maybe this was just sympathy. Or, maybe all those jokes I'd played hiding backpacks had paid off? Maybe the pranks on the football team had worked? Perhaps the girls did love me, like their texts after the assembly had said. Probably just sympathy, though.

When I was at my lowest point, my twin had had to give a speech *for* me and *about* me while I locked myself away. Now I dared to speak in front of everyone about my issues. Mr. Culley, Mrs. Margraf, and Sean saved me at the assembly. Those fifteen minutes not only shaped my outlook on life but made me a much happier person. Instead of daydreaming about life without FA, I could live and prosper *with* FA. People knew the real me, and I didn't have to keep any more secrets. I knew it was my time to publicly open up about my struggles. But how would I convey my story so people could take something from it?

What would I want to say to my classmates, their siblings, and their grandparents? What *should* I say? I considered that maybe some people saw a flicker of inspiration in me. Perhaps seeing my struggle and pain had taught them not to sweat the small stuff. The way I'd decided not to complain after hearing stories about people like Travis Roy, maybe my classmates had chosen not to complain after seeing me try as hard as I could to stay positive.

I dove deep into my speech. The message would be about dreaming big, accepting when the dream is interrupted by something you can't control, and being willing to create a new dream. Randy Pausch said, "It's not about how to achieve your dreams; it's about how to live your life." We need to assess our lives, adapt to changes, and pivot into discovering new dreams. That is not giving up on the dream, but developing something new. I wanted—no, I *needed*—to tell the audience that through struggle and pain come beauty and peace.

My dream, until I was thirteen, had been to be the next Kobe Bryant. That dream vanished in the blink of an eye. No matter how hard I tried to get that dream back, no matter how much I kicked, screamed, hid, pitied myself, or resented the world, it was gone. For years, I struggled, I hurt, and I wondered if I would ever be able to dream big again. I would explain that FA would always be a major roadblock in my life but that I would always do everything in my power to not let it stop me. Just because I couldn't be the next Kobe Bryant of the NBA didn't mean I couldn't be the next Joey Mullaney of my life, attacking challenges with what Kobe called the "Mamba Mentality."

When my old dream was destroyed, I became afraid of the world. I was a scared kid going to a new high school, changing myself to make new friends, managing a basketball team instead of playing on it, hiding my disease, allowing Sean to handle my fears, having friends question if I was okay, and crying in Coach Kev's class.

Randy Pausch also said, "Experience is what you got when you didn't get what you wanted. And experience is often the most valuable thing you have to offer." I did not want FA, but the experience of coping with the disease led me into another world in which I was no longer afraid—a magical reality in which I was slam-dunking basketballs and going viral online, sailing the Caribbean, addressing the student body in a public speech at high school graduation, and going off to dorm away at college.

Seeing the graduation setup—the tent, stage, tables, podium, microphone, and chairs—made my speech feel real. I was up with my classmates at 4:30 a.m. that day so we could all witness our final sunrise sitting together on the football field—an LA senior-class tradition. A few hours later, we dressed in our graduation garb before our 10 a.m. start. Shortly after the ceremony began, I was escorted to the podium by Sean and our classmate Bradley. Bradley grabbed me a chair, and Sean helped me sit and put my three-page speech on the podium. I sat there, looked out at the sea of hundreds of people, took a deep breath (from my diaphragm), and gave a big smile. "Hi, I'm Joey Mullaney. It's no surprise you all chose me since I would've been valedictorian anyway with my 4.2 GPA ..." And so it began with the crowd laughing. It felt as if I were meant to do this. I had finally found my way.

It was clear that when I got to college, I'd be off my feet for good, permanently relegated to a motorized scooter. This progression was FA in all its glory. My physical decline over the last four years couldn't be denied. But I wanted desperately to walk across that stage when my name was called and stand eye to eye with our headmaster as he shook my hand. Graduation became known in my mind as The Big Fight. I went to the gym every day for two months to strengthen my legs to get across that stage: leg-press machine, core machines, abductor and adductor machines, calf machine, you name it.

In the graduation line, I had one perk, of course: Sean. He would be called right after me. He has always been my crutch, but this time he would be one in a literal sense. The last time he was up on that stage, he was defending me, doing what I could not do by announcing to the student body that I had a deadly disease. Now, here he was as we commenced the rest of our lives. Sean and I walked arm and arm up the steps to the stage. Sean naturally thought he would help me, but I knew deep inside that I needed to grab that diploma. It looked like a baton, and it was being handed off to me, and me alone. "Joseph Mullaney," my headmaster said as people cheered. I then looked over at Sean, who was standing, as he always was, right next to me. "I got this," I told him.

When a graduate moves the tassel on his mortarboard from right to left, it symbolizes a crossing over from one stage of life to the next. For me, everything that day—inside and out—shifted in some way. It was the first time I thought I could one day help others overcome adversity, the first time I thought about writing a book and doing public speaking to fight FA as much as possible. I accepted that FA would not stop progressing, but I planned to progress, too, as long as I was still living.

PART III

The Quest

CHAPTER 22

The Irony of Independence

"I'll FaceTime you when I'm done moving in," I said to Sean and my Mom, as they helped me pack to head off to my new home in a few days. Sean and I had shared hundreds of breakfasts before rushing off to school, a practice, or a game, but this time was different. For the first time, I was leaving home for a while, and my twin wasn't joining me. Sean and my mom drove north to school in Maine, while my dad and I went south to school in Connecticut.

The decision to leave Massachusetts was my own. There are great schools in Massachusetts. Nobody was forcing me to leave the comforts of home. My parents would have been perfectly happy and supportive of my decision to stay home. Every chance she had, my mom raved about the colleges within thirty miles of us and how I would love them.

But I was curious about the kind of life I could make for myself if I were on my own. Who would become my friends? How would I act in the face of challenges? What would it be like to have to do my own laundry? How would I be able to fold and put away my clothes with FA, the illness that was causing me to lose my hand-eye coordination? Could I accomplish everyday tasks without my family and friends?

Truthfully, the scariest thing of all was my decision to stop walking permanently. Not that you could call what I was doing that summer walking, exactly. FA had progressed quickly, and by the end of summer, I was stumbling, really struggling to walk without help. Let's just say I leaned against, or fell into, a lot of walls and relied on my upper-body strength to hold me up and save me from eating it. I could not handle any more panicking fiascos in college like what had gone down at Rachel's Sweet Sixteen party or in my driver's ed course. Those eye-opening experiences taught me I couldn't go off to college walking like it was the zombie apocalypse.

Just like every college freshman, I wanted to become independent. I did not want to worry about walking from my bed to the bathroom and falling helplessly to the floor. I was looking forward to the "normal" worries every college kid has, like getting to class thirty minutes early to get a front-row seat, finishing assignments weeks before they are due, and getting to the library by 6:30 p.m. every Friday to do homework for four hours. (Yeah, right! If you've read this book from the beginning, you know by now that I'm full of it.) It was time to trade in my faulty legs for a three-wheeled motorized scooter—with a headlight!

With the scooter, getting around anywhere would be so much easier. I'd be able to hang up my towel after a shower without having to prop myself against the sink to do so. I could hold a conversation while heading across campus without losing my breath, and I wouldn't need to allow an extra twenty minutes to walk slowly. And who knows! Maybe I'd even try drinking hot coffee again. My hands had gotten so weak and shaky from FA that the last time I had coffee, I'd lost my grip and scorched myself. I ended up with third-degree burns all over my hands and a scarring memory. (Baby ~~steps~~ scoots, Joe, baby scoots.)

The summer before QU was the first time I went scooter shopping at the medical supply store. You would've thought I was twelve years old again walking into an Apple store. My eyes lit up at the rows and rows of ingenious gadgets that could instantly make my life so much easier. The medical supply store was my very own tech heaven, where instead of drooling over the latest iPhone, I got excited about the cell phone holder that attaches to a scooter, an attachable cup holder, and even the twenty-six-inch hand-grip reacher rod!

"Oh my goodness! I'll take one of everything!" I told my parents, who said no, just the scooter. My sister and parents had become regular customers at the medical supply store by now. The store owner loved Kaela and already knew all about me, even though I'd never met him. As we exited, I imagined how much freedom the scooter was going to give me once I got to college.

I can proudly say with confidence that I am awful at driving a car. I lose focus way too often, and if one of Luke Bryan's new songs comes on the radio, I turn the volume up too high and sing like a wannabe Ariana Grande. I could take the easy route and blame it on being from Massachusetts, where most drivers have road rage, but that's an excuse. The reality is I'm just a bad driver. Once when I was driving the Black Mamba, I was late for school and ran a red trying to beat it—right in front of a cop. I didn't even wait for his siren; I just pulled myself over and handed him my registration and driver's license. When there wasn't a traffic light getting me into trouble, there were plenty of snow banks. There wasn't a snow bank I hadn't met. The idea of me driving a scooter made some of the people who love me wince.

I chose the same brand of motorized scooter that my sister uses: Pride Mobility. My model is bigger because I am almost a foot taller than Kaela. When I took it for a test drive at home, I had that new-car feeling. I was excited to drive it and see what my new toy could do. I spent that summer testing out my new whip.

There was something cartoonish about it. Instead of a speedometer, I have a knob that turns left toward an image of a turtle, or right toward an image of a bunny. The turtle represents the slowest mode, one mile per hour. The bunny is the fastest speed, a blistering seven miles per hour. I can adjust the knob to go anywhere between turtle and bunny.

To put it into non-disabled person terms, I now moved as fast as an easy stroll in the park on turtle or a light jog on bunny. I can't tell you how much you can underestimate seven miles per hour, especially while you're sitting down. I nearly gave myself whiplash the first time I turned to bunny mode. It was beyond wicked awesome, even though my parents lost their cool on me.

"The speed limit in the house is at the halfway point from turtle to bunny, Joseph! (I'm only referred to by my full name when I'm in trouble.) Stop screaming that you're Ricky Bobby and like to go fast!"

Bunny mode comes in handy, though—I can pee just when the Red Sox are changing pitchers! Turtle mode, on the other hand, is so damn slow. It's like waiting for the next drip to come out of a leaky faucet or being stuck behind a person "enjoying the scenery" at the mall as you're racing to the bathroom after chugging a forty-ounce soda.

The three-hour drive down Interstate 95 to Quinnipiac was tense. My older cousin had just gotten hitched. The day after her wedding, I said my goodbyes and left for my first day of college during the post-wedding brunch. My mom stayed behind. While she teared up hugging me goodbye in the parking lot, she kept reminding me to have fun and stay safe.

The closer we got to QU, the more my dad tensed up. As he gripped the wheel, he went into Dad mode and reeled off a list of reminders for me:

"Call often and get to class early."

"Okay, Dad."

"Don't try to do it all on your own. It's okay to ask for help, Joey."

"I know, Dad."

"Don't make me your mother and I grandparents yet please."

"Understood, Dad. Got it."

"Don't be a hothead, either."

"I won't be, Dad."

"Don't be a wise guy to your professors."

"ME?! NEVER!"

"Don't drink too much, don't drink and drive on your scooter, don't let anyone on your scooter, call your mother, FaceTime us, rest when you need to, don't apply for any credit cards, make wise decisions, and don't forget to call us if you need anything. ... You still certain about this, Joe?"

"Dad! Yes," I answered, giving him a reassuring smile.

"I'm not kidding, Joey. This is serious. Study and be safe."

During the long car ride, I noticed that my dad kept answering phone calls every fifteen minutes. He just kept responding with, "Yes, uh-huh, will do, got it." Years later, I discovered those phone calls were from my mom. Mom kept telling Dad to give me all that advice. And not to let me know she was on the phone. Mom also wanted Dad to put a family picture on my new night-stand so I would see my parents every night before I went to bed.

Dad and I unpacked and made my bed, and soon after, we both stood there, waiting for the long goodbye. "Soooo ... okay," he said with teary eyes as he went in for a hug.

"I'm gonna be okay, Dad," I said. My stomach turned over. "You can go." I was getting emotional, but I knew he would have withdrawn me from school if I began to cry.

"I'll call you tomorrow before class," he said.

Dad hugged and kissed me on the cheek, as only a father could. Watching him walk out the door, and me sitting in my scooter, I suddenly felt "independent." *That* feeling hit me hard and was way too real for my liking. In my head, the running script was, *"Oh, wait ... this is happening."*

QU Residential Services paired every new student with a random roommate. Mine was a big, ex-high school football kid from Rhode Island named Mike C.

After QU informed me a month before school that Mike C. would be my roommate, I knew I had to tell him about my situation. It would not have been cool if I'd talked to him for the first time on move-in day, and he was like, "Uhhhh, QU, what is going on?!" So, that summer I anxiously messaged him to inform him of my scooter situation. I was so nervous about how he would take it, but it turned out he didn't mind at all. Mike C. ended our chat on Facebook Messenger by saying, "... as long as you enjoy having a good time." We were a solid match.

The morning classes began, I awoke to my alarm with a smile on my face. Seeing a framed photo of my family on my nightstand made me feel ready. I got up early to give myself enough time to get ready, eat, and make it to class minutes before everyone else. My first-floor dorm room was roughly a seven-minute scoot to the cafeteria (on half-speed). The cafeteria was inside a large building, half of which housed classrooms, science labs, a bookstore, A SLOW AND TINY ELEVATOR, and various other meeting rooms and offices. The other half held the cafeteria, which featured one floor of food stations and seating and a second story for extra seating.

I was so excited to eat my first college meal. But after I entered the building and headed to the cafeteria, I discovered I couldn't get in! The entrance had three turnstiles. There wasn't an automated door button or a sign saying how someone in a scooter or a wheelchair could enter.

How did I miss this on my tour? I probably should not have focused so much on the older, beautiful women ...

I couldn't embarrass myself on day one, but I needed to eat. I weighed my options: Either pout and starve, or figure out another solution and move on. I chose the latter, so I stayed calm and searched. I suddenly understood why people say you often learn more *outside* of the classroom in college.

I went back outside and scooted around the building to see if there was another entrance. No luck. When I went back indoors, I eventually found the spot where students checked out at the registers. That would be my opening!

BOOM! I'M IN!

As others exited, I entered. And that was how I got to breakfast, lunch, and dinner every day throughout my years at QU.

I'd officially overcome my first obstacle at college.

See, Mom and Dad? Nothing to worry about.

People on campus quickly noticed my scooter. I'd crank it up leaving my dorm and be in class at least ten minutes before anyone else arrived. I was friendly to people, usually engaging them first so I could offset their stares. I quickly became a phenomenal small-talk conversationalist. It had been a while since I'd had to explain FA to anyone. My conversation with Mike C. had been online. Now, I'd be starting all over with people who didn't know me, and the thought of being asked a bunch of questions, without Sean or my family answering them for me, gave me anxiety. It takes a lot to explain to someone new that you have a genetic condition that continuously weakens every muscle down to your toes and up to your skull. That particular conversation takes a level of trust I didn't have with many people.

"So, why do you use the scooter?" was the most popular question I fielded. If I was already in a great conversation with someone, I'd tell them the truth. If not, I had an arsenal full of comical responses. "Well," I'd say, "I was in a bad bobsledding accident last week." Or, "I was in a serious downhill skiing accident three days ago." I'd get massive kicks out of seeing the perplexed looks on people's faces when they realized it was September and seventy-two degrees. Occasionally, if the questioner was someone I didn't want to talk to, I'd leave them very confused by saying, "You should see the other guy!"

Despite having met several cool kids around campus, by October I missed my squad back home. Things were more challenging than usual for me. Although I'd made friends, I didn't have anyone to lean on—literally and figuratively. I got tired more quickly, and that frustrated me. Sean and I talked a lot, but it was still weird and unsettling to have my twin not know what was going on with me every day, and vice versa. And to make it all worse, the novelty of my scooter wore off after a month. Even bunny mode failed to give me the adrenaline rush I craved.

One Sunday afternoon, I headed back to my dorm after grabbing food from the cafeteria across campus. I was scooting down Bobcat Way, the main road through QU that ended at my dorm, when I realized I'd forgotten silverware. Afraid to miss the Patriots' kickoff, I ripped my scooter into bunny mode while making a sharp U-turn, and BOOM! The right side of my body and my scooter abruptly met the pavement.

It's difficult to put into words what it feels like to be on the ground and unable to move. It's even harder to describe the feeling of helplessness when you're immobile on a college campus on a quiet, lonely Sunday. My mind wandered to the fact that a buddy or Sean would've been with me at home, and I wouldn't have been in this mess. I didn't know what to do. While one part of my brain was going into unbaked soft pretzel mode to figure my way out of this, another part of me grasped something like never before. At that exact moment, I realized my scooter wasn't just a cool toy. It was a necessity, and I would be dependent on it for the rest of my life.

I lay there in the street, hoping I could find a way to get up. Just when I thought it couldn't get any worse, along came a beautiful girl. I hadn't formally met Emily before, but I knew of her because she was, well, hard not to notice.

"Jeez, are you all right?!" she asked with worry in her voice. She had seen me flip over and had run down the Way to get to me.

"Well …" was the best I could come up with as I turned fifty shades of red. Emily, who didn't know I knew her, actually laughed as she got my scooter upright. As I lay on the ground, she picked up my scooter, reconnected the twenty-pound battery that also had fallen off, and then helped me back on.

I had to give her props for helping me get back on, since I was about 150 pounds of dead weight. "This thing is much heavier than it looks," Emily said as sweat begin to drip off her forehead.

"Err, sorry about that," I managed to say. "The scooter's diet starts tomorrow." I had to make a joke somehow, so Emily wouldn't worry about me. I was super grateful but still trying to figure out how to keep my man card.

I began to hurry away when I looked back and said, "Thank you, Emily. Next time I'll try not to tip over." When she giggled, I decided my impaired driving had finally come in handy.

I might be okay here, after all.

CHAPTER 23

The Scooter Socialite

'm not going to lie. I didn't bounce back right away from the incident on Bobcat Way. Yes, I mean, I physically bounced back, thanks to Emily. And I was encouraged that people would help me and then not make it the school's gossip. But the weight of the scooter on top of me began to feel like an emotional burden. The reality had hit: Wheels have replaced my legs, and this disease *is* progressing. I freaked out.

What will the other kids think of me?

Will professors treat me how my middle school teacher did when she learned I have FA?

Will anyone sit with me in the cafeteria?

When it begins snowing, how will I get to class from my dorm?

Will anyone talk to me?

Will my dormmates like me?

Will I be able to survive on my own, without Sean?

Will the kids treat me as Joey? Or will I be treated like the kid you feel bad for and don't know how to act around?

Will people start screaming "HELLO!" to me, wearing giant smiles, even though I can hear just fine?

It turned out that kids, or young adults, in college are (somewhat) mature and make things strange only if you let them. So, I learned to control how people treated me. I acted like any other student, and I was confident, which encouraged people to befriend me.

Two doors down from my dorm room was a room full of guys I clicked with. Jon Nanna, whom everyone called Nanna, was a stocky guy from New Jersey with short hair that he gelled up in the front. He was friendly and outgoing, always the life of the party. Being a diehard New York Giants fan, he graciously reminded me (constantly) that the Giants had beaten the Patriots in the Super Bowl.

Then there was Mike Rocco. Everyone called him Rocco, but for this story, to distinguish him from my old friend, I'll refer to him as Mike. Mike was a skinny guy from Staten Island with a faded buzz cut. He has the best New York accent. He sounds like Joe Pesci in *My Cousin Vinny*. Mike was pretty quiet until we watched NFL games together on Sundays. Then he wouldn't stop talking about how awful the New York Jets are.

Lastly, there was Matt Blumenthal, whom everyone called Bloomy. He was a skinny ginger with a buzz cut and glasses. He is from San Francisco, and his laidback attitude proves it. Bloomy enjoys trying different things, so hopping on a seven-hour plane ride from home to QU was nothing out of the ordinary for him.

As we were getting to know one another, we kept overhearing older students around campus talking about a club named Toad's in New Haven. Toad's had two floors and four bars—three smaller bars on the first floor and a large bar on the second floor. Each level had a giant dance floor. It was a legendary club, everyone said. All we heard about was the dancing, drinking, laughing, and then more drinking. Monday through Wednesday and again on Friday nights, Toad's was open to everyone. Yale students reserved the place on Thursday nights. Saturday nights, the club turned into "Quinnipiac University Night." QU even had shuttle buses, policed by members of QU Campus Safety.

Usually, two campus safety officers sat on the bus to monitor the dozens of excited college kids, making sure nobody got sick or became too obnoxious and unruly.

After my new buddies and I prepared for the night, I scooted my way to the front of the rec center with them to board the shuttle. There were about thirty of us freshmen, loud and obnoxious. The dress code at Toad's was simple: Dress to impress. No Timberlands, no chains, and no hats. The girls wore their best skinny black pants or dresses with either wedges or heels, while the boys wore collared shirts or button-downs with khaki pants and boat shoes.

When I arrived, I waved to my new friend Patty, the campus safety officer on duty. She headed over to speak with the shuttle driver. As they were talking, I saw the shuttle had a lift in the back to get my scooter on. But for some reason, steel chains gated up the lift. I overheard Patty's conversation with the shuttle driver: "I'm sorry for that kid, but there's some operational error and it's not working."

Sweet! That's awesome! I can't wait to sit alone in my dorm room and play video games while my new friends dance the night away!

I looked up in line at my new buddy, Nanna, and said with sadness that I couldn't go anymore. He seemed confused, but the inaccessible cafeteria entrance and now the shuttle were my new normal. Nanna signaled to a few of our other buddies. Then he told me to get on his back while the other guys lifted my scooter onto the shuttle. The shuttle driver and Patty both watched in amazement. I couldn't wait anymore for the night—and for the rest of the year. I had terrific new friends by my side.

When we arrived at Toad's, it was immediate chaos, the most extraordinary kind. Music was blaring, fog machines were spraying dry ice all around, drinks were flowing, and people were dancing everywhere. Whenever I spoke to a girl, I would say Tom Brady was my cousin, then show her the picture of me with him during my Make-A-Wish day a few months earlier. That dumb pickup move failed that night and again for many other nights throughout the years.

Idk, I thought it would work.

On a summer day in 2013, before I left for QU, the Make-A-Wish Foundation had coordinated a day for me to meet the entire New England Patriots team before one of their training camp practices. Although Make-A-Wish warned me I would probably be one of thirty wish-kids there, I didn't care. I wanted to meet my heroes.

In the end, I ended up being the only kid there.

I used a wheelchair, because I could still stand and walk, but only for a short amount of time. My family and I waited outside the locker room to greet the players before they ran onto the practice field.

I'd followed the Patriots obsessively all my life, but seeing them exit their locker room one by one to greet my family and me was the first moment I realized how big these guys are. It was evident to me that you have to either be a large animal or a gigantic monster to play in the NFL. The size of these beasts—who were all in amazing shape with tons of athletic ability—was insane.

After I'd met most of the team, there were still two Patriots I had yet to encounter. As I turned toward the tunnel, I saw in the distance a Greek god-like figure—the most beautiful man I've ever seen. The glorious Thomas Edward Brady was walking toward me. A choir of angels surrounded him as he walked. I hopped out of my chair as TB12 greeted me graciously with a big bear hug and handed me a bag. The bag included a customized Patriots jersey and other memorable gifts, including a friendly letter from the team owner, Robert Kraft. Adrenaline and excitement helped strengthen my legs.

When I saw TB12 in the flesh, I honestly forgot the English language. Like an idiot, I just stared at him. Eventually, we took pictures together despite my dumbfoundedness. As I was standing with Tom—we're on a first-name basis now, obviously—I felt someone come up next to me and tap my shoulder. Oh, it was just Coach Belichick. No big deal.

What is happening?! My head was exploding.

"Ooh, hey, Coach Belichick, how are you?" was my best response, as if we were old buddies catching up.

As I talked to my two new best friends, I suddenly got a sinking feeling. Literally. Adrenaline could sustain my weakening legs for only so long. I'd been standing for quite some time, and my legs had had enough. I was going down.

My family, meanwhile, was just as starstruck. So even though they were watching this close encounter among the three amigos, they didn't notice me wobbling and starting to lose my balance. (Who can blame them, though? Have I mentioned how radiant Tom is?)

I was sure I was going down face-first into the turf, right in front of my soulmate. But instead, I felt a firm hand grab my arm, steadying me and keeping me upright.

I had been saved! And by none other than good ol' TB12 himself. Just as he's done in so many late-game comebacks, Tom Brady had performed yet another miracle I'll never forget.

Even though he couldn't help me get a date once I got to college, I genuinely love the man.

My QU friends and I started going to Toad's every week. We developed our own routine. The upstairs bar had a particular table where my buddies would plant me for the night. The chair was high enough so I was at eye level with everyone. I could finally have a conversation and be able to hear what other people were saying without craning my neck.

But the novelty of going to Toad's every Saturday started to wear off after a few weeks. Toad's was still a place we wanted to go, but we figured we'd get more out of it if our squad grew. We decided we wanted more, something different.

CHAPTER 24

ADA-Accessible Greek House

When you stop partying and come out of your dazed and confused state, it hits you hard in the face: These classes are challenging! Winter break couldn't have come at a better time. Regrouping was what I needed, and living at home for a few weeks would help me rest my body and brain. At home, my new buddies and I kept in touch through a group chat.

Nanna:

It's freezing here in Jersey.

I'm so bored at home...I miss QU.

I miss the freedom.

Bloomy:

It's 75 and sunny here in California.

I told you all to come visit!

Mike:

New York is so damn cold too, Nanna.

My house is full of screaming Italians, chicken cutlets, rice balls, and annoying twelve-year-old girls since my little sister needs to have her loud friends over all the time...

I need a wild night when we all get back.

Me:

Mass is brutally cold. Sean already went back to school for baseball season. Being home alone with my parents sucks. I can't wait to see you boys again :)

Bloomy:

So I'm excited to see you guys at the SigEp rush events this semester!

Mike:

Bloomy, the three of us told you we r not gonna rush.

Bloomy:

Just come to one rush event, guys! Then, if you all don't like it, I'll let you all split a Large Buffalo Chicken Pie from Marvino's on me.

Me:

Say no more. Deal.

Nanna:

For only one event, why not?

Mike:

For a free Pie?!?!
In.

After that conversation ended, I went straight into my dad's office in our house to ask what he thought about me joining a fraternity. At first, he was hesitant, saying how reckless frats are and how my grades would suffer. My dad had the idea that every fraternity was full of young men who only partied. That was it. But hearing from Bloomy and other buddies I knew from class or met around campus, I understood that notion was a fallacy. Yes, fraternities do indeed party. But they also pride themselves on having academic success, ensuring each member has a strong moral character, participating in philanthropic events, and achieving the best after college. I explained how fraternities are not like they were when Dad was in college in the 1970s. I told him how Bloomy was already in and that I'd rush with Nanna and Mike.

Although Dad wasn't on board, he loved and trusted my new college buddies, so he was okay with me attending a rush event to see if I'd like it. Years later, I found out my mom had talked Dad into it. Even though Dad felt it would be too much work for me, Mom thought it would give me a great sense of community.

The QU administration wanted Greek life on campus, but they didn't want it to get out of control, with 24/7 partying. They didn't want students to drink so much they were just wasting away their college experience (and their money). To keep things controlled, each student in a Greek organization had to maintain a GPA of 2.5 or better. There were a dozen different fraternities and sororities, but none had a house on campus. Off campus, houses were deemed "Greek houses" if four to six members of an organization lived there together. But they were ordinary homes, nothing like the mansions you see in the South.

If you weren't part of a Greek organization, you were not often allowed at the house. And fraternities and sororities were required to hold rush events on campus. A few weeks into the spring semester, Nanna, Mike, and I decided to go to the first rush event put on by Bloomy's fraternity, Sigma Phi Epsilon, or SigEp for short.

The first event was overwhelming. A hundred-something guys stood around in one of the business lecture halls on campus, making small talk. Rush events are essentially twenty to thirty prospective brothers, like us three, talking with as many of the brothers as we could. Each member had one vote on the rushees: yes or no. So, we talked all night to make a member like us and want us in their fraternity. I call this man-flirting, meaning we had to compliment the brothers and ask questions that boosted their egos.

"Wow, no way! You have a great GPA and had a winter internship at XYZ company, and they might offer you a full-time position once you graduate?! That's incredible! I'm failing at Subject X 101 or IThinkThisIsWorking 301. Do you mind tutoring me sometime?" I'd say with glee, over and over again.

Then the lights flickered, and ten of the older guys walked to the front of the room while the other brothers stood surrounding the rushees. SigEp's recruitment chair gave an introductory speech and spoke about how SigEp positively changes lives. He explained how each brother discovers how to have a sound mind and sound body, and each brother lives by SigEp's founding principles: virtue, diligence, and brotherly love.

He followed his speech by playing a video on the projector in the lecture hall. The four-minute video featured snippets of brothers attending philanthropic activities, images of their black-tie event, and highlights of their academic strengths. The clip made it well known that SigEp had the highest cumulative GPA among all the fraternities at QU.

After the video ended, the brothers erupted in cheers until the walls shook. That camaraderie reminded me of how close I was to all my teammates growing up. I had not realized how much I loved and missed that bond until that scene. I knew I needed to get in.

After that night, there were three more rush events we could attend. The final event was a formal dinner put on by the brothers, and it was invitation-only. Only half the rushees were invited, but the three of us made the cut. We all dressed as sharply as we could, wearing the best suits we had. Lucky for me, I'd had to get a new navy suit for my cousin's wedding.

That dinner made me feel closer to the brothers. Many of them let their guards down and talked more sincerely with me. One brother discussed his troubles at school; another spoke about how much he loved being at QU because his home life was toxic. At the first rush events, those guys barely gave a rushee the time of day as they stood up straight with cocky grins. After dinner, I would have to wait a few days to learn if I'd gotten in.

One night, Mike, Nanna, a few of our buddies, and I journeyed to Toad's for what we hoped would be our final trip as non-Greek men. It was a cold and snowy February night. Nanna pushed me in my wheelchair as we made our way to the shuttles. I didn't like going out in my scooter anymore after seeing my buddies have to carry both me and it onto a shuttle for our first trip to Toad's. The wheelchair I had was light and easy to fold up, so it served as my new transportation when I went to the bar.

The line for the shuttle was crowded, and we froze as we waited to get aboard. That's when a group of six obnoxious, older-looking boys behind us caused a stir. (They looked like they'd already done plenty of pregaming.) One of the annoying loud-mouths started jumping around to heat up. Without knowing or caring, he bumped into me and tipped my chair over, sending me into a snow bank.

Oh, shit!

Immediately, Nanna and Mike telepathically agreed to divide and conquer. Mike and a group of girls in line ran over to help me up, while Nanna and a few of our other buddies confronted the guy and his goon squad. The campus safety officers broke up the scuffle before things got serious and sent us all back to our dorms.

Once we got back inside and started replaying the previous twenty minutes, we began worrying that SigEp wouldn't take us because of the incident. But the fact was, there was nothing we could do but wait for tomorrow.

The next morning, we received knocks on our doors from a SigEp brother offering us bids. Once we all accepted our bids, the brother said the scuffle had turned out to be a good thing. One of the calmer boys in that rambunctious group the night before was a member of SigEp. He'd explained the story to the entire organization—including how his friend had started the mess. He even told them that Nanna and Mike were just defending me, showing brotherly love.

When you accept a bid from SigEp, you are automatically a brother. But you still have to earn the respect of each member throughout the semester. The first couple of months are like a probationary period. Each Sunday, the entire brotherhood meets as a chapter to discuss any business relating to the fraternity. New members like me did not speak unless we had important news. The five members of the Executive Board (E-Board) sat in front of the conference room, facing the other hundred members. They would take turns speaking to the rest of the chapter.

The discussions at chapter would include updates on philanthropic events and parties, brothers' GPAs, and callouts if a brother had misbehaved. If you fell below a 2.5, the vice president of fraternal standards sent you to a meeting with the Standards Committee. To reinforce proper behavior at parties or on campus, that brother had to apologize in front of the entire chapter. We reflected well on one another, so that wasn't too much of a concern. I found that we all did a pretty good job being brothers.

I had gained the infamous Freshman Fifteen. Being able to order yourself Domino's cheesy bread every night, sitting in a scooter for thirteen hours a day, and drinking beer four to five times a week will do that to you.

Having FA, I knew I had to exercise if I wanted to live a longer life. With FA, the muscles atrophy at twice the speed of a person without FA. "Use them or lose them," my neurologist told me many times. The reason I had begun working out years prior was more than to just make me better at basketball. It was to prevent my muscles from atrophying. I fell out of my exercise regimen in college, so I knew I needed to get back into fighting shape and on the right track. My life was literally at stake.

For years, I had dealt with FA the best way I knew how to: by avoiding it. Up until the scooter, I hadn't zeroed in on the gravity of it all. It was too hard to do, emotionally. When I would say to myself, "Deal with the pain of falling in the shower," or, "Deal with scooting away on bunny mode after dropping my iced tea bottle in front of a beautiful girl standing behind me in line at the cafeteria," I really meant, "Keep distracting yourself from FA's progression." Now, I was starting to understand that my body was retaliating. My feet were numb, and my legs didn't move well. My upper-body function was still unafflicted. As my dad and brother taught me in middle school, working out my upper body would help me get around more easily. Exercising made transferring to and from my scooter, opening doors, and bouncing around on campus to see friends much more comfortable—and hopefully slowed the progression of FA.

The summer after freshman year at QU, I needed to exercise. I followed my mom to join our town's CrossFit gym. I was becoming exhausted during the school day and falling more often when transferring. Something needed to change.

Mom is an excellent CrossFit athlete who performs as if she's thirty years younger. She has competed against—and defeated—some of the best athletes around the country in several competitions. Mom introduced me to the gym's trainer, Nick, who was energetic, kind, and determined. Even though he knew a little about FA from my family's history, he never went easy on me. We worked out two to three times a week, while both learning everything we could about FA along the way.

CrossFit's workouts of the day (WODs) made me feel physically and emotionally invincible. I will admit, I almost quit after week two because it exhausted me. But before I had the chance to try something else, I came across Steph Hammerman on Instagram. Steph has cerebral palsy (CP) and does Adaptive CrossFit exercises, meaning she does various CrossFit WODs but adapts them to her body's needs and abilities. She believes Adaptive CrossFit is helping save her life. Since Adaptive CrossFit was helping her battle with CP, I thought it might help me battle FA. So I stuck with it.

Nick had me bench pressing and doing pushups, pullups, situps, squats, calf raises, and Olympic lifts to my ability. He assisted me as I stood up out of my chair to walk ten steps forward and ten steps back. I did battle ropes while sitting in my scooter, and I even hopped onto a stationary bike and pedaled. It almost seemed as if Nick wanted me to cry. To go along with exercising, Nick helped me focus on my nutrition. I tried to eat less fast food and looked for proteins to boost energy and build muscle. Daily omega-3s, amino acids, and calcium became part of my arsenal.

By the end of summer, heading back to QU for my sophomore year, I could do pullups with my wheelchair attached to me. I even grew a four-pack of abs, which is enormous. For someone sitting in a scooter all day, developing a four-pack is equivalent to an eight-pack on an able-bodied person. Many young people don't begin paying attention to their physical health until they've abused their bodies thoroughly. I feel lucky to have gotten the memo early to treat my body as a temple—one of the ironic gifts of having FA.

CHAPTER 25

Virtue, Diligence, and Brotherly Love

"Your EKG results came back better than ever! The levels from both your left and right ventricle hypertrophic cardiomyopathy have significantly decreased since I last saw you six months ago," said my cardiologist, Dr. Daniels. According to heart.org, hypertrophic cardiomyopathy is a disease that makes it harder for your heart to pump blood to the rest of your body. My heart issues did not occur until my early years in college, but I knew when I was thirteen that hypertrophic cardiomyopathy would come. On top of that, aggressive scoliosis, energy loss, muscle fatigue, heart arrhythmias, and diabetes are prevalent symptoms of FA. Not every FA patient develops those symptoms, but most do.

During my previous six-month checkup, I was just joining SigEp, barely exercising (if at all), and partying and eating like a typical college freshman. I explained to my cardiologist how I had been exercising more frequently and treating my body like a temple over the summer. "Well, Joey, whatever you've been doing, keep doing it!" Dr. Daniels said with excitement. "On your way out, please schedule an appointment in six months, and I'll see you then."

"Before I go, Dr. Daniels, I was wondering if there are any types of medication that are safe for my heart and could help increase my energy throughout the day. I feel like I could fall back asleep multiple times a day, and I don't even do many activities during a typical day."

"I'm not aware of any at the moment. I'll talk to some of my colleagues around the hospitals in Boston and see, Joe."

On the days I worked out at QU's recreational center, I would be extra tired. A light, five-minute cardio exercise on a stationary bike exhausted me. I would move more slowly when I had to shower, change, prepare my meals, and go to class. I felt like I was constantly trying not to fall asleep in class or while socializing with people in the cafeteria, doing homework, and spending time with friends in my dorm.

Being a brother in SigEp put an end to the loneliness and fear I felt that first semester at QU. When you have a disability, you can feel like the only person in a room, lonely in your fight. You fear that if an accident happens, you'll be completely helpless; in my case, I could even die. But now, whenever I slipped in the shower or needed help folding my clothes, preparing my meals, or carrying food in the cafeteria, my brothers were there to help. Our fraternity preaches virtue, diligence, and brotherly love, and it was refreshing to see it practicing what it preached.

Once I let people know about FA, they sometimes ask me if there is a cure or treatment. The straight answer is a big fat *NO*, but that has never stopped me from exercising, eating right, and staying on top of clinical trials and new research on medications. I mostly do this through the Friedreich's Ataxia Research Alliance (FARA), a nonprofit organization dedicated to supporting those afflicted with FA and pursuing scientific research that will lead to treatments and a cure.

During one of my dreams, I was awakened in the middle of the night in my dorm room by football's G.O.A.T, Tom Brady. I opened my eyes and abruptly sat up. I said, "Tom ... I mean, handsome ... I mean, Mr. Brady! How you been, dude?!" But he didn't respond. He grabbed my hand and walked with me outside my dorm. Outside was now the empty beach, located in front of the hotel in Aruba. Tom stopped, looked at me, and handed me two pills. As I went to grab them, he closed his hand and pulled his arm away. He said his only words: "Run for a deep pass along the shore and catch your future." I obeyed my leader and ran along the shore as fast as I could. As the pills were on their descent into my hands, I woke with sweat dripping down my forehead, lying in my bed in my dorm with my scooter beside my bed frame.

It was hard not to get my hopes up. How could I not dream of the day?

I came across one particular research trial that excited me. It was the first article I'd seen about a promising treatment. Up to that point, I did not enjoy reading articles about FA. I was so exhausted from hearing doctors say they were working on treatments and cures. "Just be patient, Joey," I'd hear at the end of every visit with my neurologist and cardiologist. FARA rarely shares articles on their Facebook page, so when they shared this one, I assumed it was promising. After reading it, I was eager to show someone.

I'd just gotten back from going into town to get a haircut when I saw the article. Sophomores were allowed to have their cars on campus, so I brought Kaela's old accessible van, which was now mine. It was an ordinary soccer mom van on the outside, but inside, the middle row of seats was gone and there was a four-foot-long automatic ramp that I could deploy to scoot in and out of the van.

I now lived with Nanna and Mike. Bloomy lived across campus but was hanging with me in our dorm's common area. I handed him my laptop so he could read what was on my screen.

"Holy shit, Joey, this is amazing!" Bloomy said, his eyes opening with intrigue. "Wow! We have to tell the guys. They'll love it!"

"Yeaahhhh, I don't know about that. But it's awesome," I replied.

I knew the guys would love it. They all loved me, and I loved them. I still had not told everyone why I'm in a scooter. Obviously they could see something wasn't right with my legs, as I sat in a scooter with long chicken legs. I didn't want to tell them and make my problem theirs, too. I was okay with people knowing about FA, since it was apparent now anyway, but I was not okay with people dealing with the same struggles, fears, and pain that I had to.

Bloomy and I had a strong friendship. He was one of my best friends now, and I told him everything.

"Joe, listen. I know you're afraid to speak in front of the guys," he said. "I know you may not think they're with you in your fight, but they are, and they want to help. They want to see FA end as much as you do! These guys can and will help you turn that pain into something positive. Just trust me, Joey."

I knew Bloomy was right. And I didn't want this to be a repeat of seventh grade when my teacher treated me differently and I played dumb to hide the truth. Thanks to Bloomy, I decided there was no good reason to hide this news.

Bloomy watched me forward the email to our fraternity president, saying I would like to speak about an FA research article in our next chapter meeting. The president responded right away, in all caps: "YES, JOEY!"

So in the next chapter, I got up in front of everyone and basically blacked out from fear. I blathered some nonsense for a few minutes before an older brother—a physical therapy major who worked with two patients with FA—graciously took the microphone from me and explained the article. After the chapter meeting, he and I spoke one-on-one. He'd had no idea I had FA. Knowing how rare FA is, he connected me with his two FA patients.

A couple of weeks after that chapter, I was home for a weekend for a doctor's appointment. Bloomy called me.

"Dude! Guess what!" he said excitedly. "SigEp at QU is switching its philanthropic efforts from Big Brothers Big Sisters of America to FARA! Now, you and I are the co-chairs assigned to organize the first event in two months!"

The event was called rideataxia+ Connecticut, and it was a 10k bike race along a path next to QU, starting and ending on campus. After the ride, there would be an outdoor reception featuring food, music, raffles, and lawn games on the quad. I had no clue about the intense responsibility that comes with co-chairing a philanthropic event. We worked with members of FARA to help us, and we spent weeks organizing everything.

First, Bloomy and I needed to spread the word about the event and our newly adopted cause. He and I met with other Greek chapters, as well as QU sports team, to encourage their participation. As co-chairs, we created plans for logistics and operations, promotion, donations, and communication and media. We assembled a team full of guys from SigEp who volunteered to help. Some guys met with the grounds crew at QU to see where we were allowed to set up shop. Others went to local restaurants to see if they would donate anything for raffles. Still other brothers created videos, flyers, and posters to share on social media and put up around campus. Some guys drove around town to find mechanical equipment to use on the day of the event.

Going into the day, we'd already collected more than $25,000 in donations.

In the process, I learned more about marketing, public speaking, strategic planning, and public relations than any of my college courses taught me.

When all was said and done, we executed a great event on a beautiful day. We had about forty people in the ride itself, with more than 250 attending the three-hour reception. Many of my hometown friends and family drove down, as well as the family with two children with FA that my SigEp brother had connected me to. We ended up raising more than $50,000 for FARA in total!

My friends and family were surprised and happy when they heard the final number. When my parents saw what we'd achieved, they got fully on board with me joining a fraternity. What will forever amaze me was the way my SigEp brothers reacted. It was pure joy—guys with wide eyes and giant smiles, hugging me and everyone else they saw. My new brothers had officially joined the war on FA. (Thank goodness I read that article!)

The unwritten rule for QU students is to hike Sleeping Giant Mountain before you graduate. The mountain is 739 feet high and overlooks the Quinnipiac campus. To hike to its peak is a rite of passage at QU. Nobody is obliged to hike it, but people will eventually discover if you didn't. Being confined to a motorized scooter, I had a pass from my peers. But just because everyone knew I couldn't go up didn't mean I didn't want to.

I wished I could take a helicopter to the peak, but I had to be realistic. I had to realize that many of the ordinary things able-bodied people do, I cannot. No longer could I walk alone to my friend's dorm room, because there were steps to get inside. I couldn't grab a Gatorade from the top shelf of the refrigerator in the cafeteria. I sometimes had to miss class if there was snowfall, because my scooter doesn't move well in snow. (Thanks to ADA laws, the school couldn't punish me for my weak scooter tires, so I wasn't marked absent and my professors emailed me the notes from class.)

Sometimes when my SigEp buddies and I were hanging around campus, they would speak of their experiences hiking the mountain. They would say, "Guys, I hiked the red trail this morning with that girl Stacy," or, "Boys, does anyone want to hike Sleeping Giant in the morning?" Hiking is an exercise, yes, but at QU, it was also a social activity.

I would always chime in with something, so I wasn't the awkward, silent kid. "Yeah, I'll meet you up there," or "I would, but my right ankle has been bothering me." These were joking lies that the boys understood. After they gave a quick laugh, they'd go silent for a minute. Without understanding the effects my words would have on them, I would say, "I'm jealous of you guys. I wish I could do it too." Then they would change the subject.

On the last Tuesday night of my sophomore year, Nanna and Mike returned from the library and came into our room to find me in bed watching Netflix. "Hey, Joe, I won a free breakfast for three on Friday at 7 a.m. at that Greek diner down the street," Nanna said. "Us three!" When you're in college and hear the word "free," it's similar to winning the lottery.

We left our room to head to the diner at 6:45. My roommates said to wear regular comfy clothing because the attire at the restaurant was casual. Nanna asked to drive my van, so I threw him my car keys. Mike rode shotgun, and I stayed in my scooter in the back. As the engine turned over, they told me to look down and not speak. Mike began blasting the new Avicii song. Every time I started to look up or ask if we were still getting blueberry pancakes, they would scream at me to stop. It was 6:50 a.m., so

I shut up. I knew something was up, but I just followed orders. That's a younger sibling/cousin quality—just go with the flow.

After a few minutes of an obnoxiously loud car ride, Nanna and Mike opened the door to let me out of the van. I saw forty of my SigEp brothers waiting for me in the parking lot of Sleeping Giant.

"So, does this mean we're not getting breakfast?" I asked. The boys laughed as our brother, Alec, came over to me. He was first up. Nanna and Mike helped me onto Alec's back. Then, they gave me a rundown of everything.

They told me how every time I said I wanted to see the top of the Sleeping Giant like everyone else at QU, they felt guilty. A few days prior, they'd all joined a private Facebook page titled "Operation Get Joey Up the Mountain." Collectively, they devised a plan. Every three to five minutes, a different brother would carry me on his back, and another brother would help me on and off safely—all while everyone ventured up the mountain.

So, beginning with Alec, that is what they did, passing me off as a human baton all in the name of getting me up that mountain. Along the way up, I had a short conversation with each brother. I began by thanking them but quickly went into sarcastic mode. I knew each brother well, so we all traded witty jokes. I teased about how fat I am to carry (I weigh 150 pounds) and bragged about how Tom Brady is undoubtedly the greatest quarterback of all time. I told them how if you say "mozzarella cheese" instead of "muzzarell che'," you can't be Italian. I asked what their summer plans were, if they had any internships lined up.

After we passed trees and marched over dirt roads, the challenging hike reached its end. Matty was carrying me last, and at the peak, he and Nick set me down to take in the view. Another brother reached into his backpack and handed each of us a beer. It was only 8 a.m., but since this was a once-in-a-lifetime experience, I happily cracked open a Bud Light with some of my best buds.

Every single day for two years, I had scooted by this beautiful peak that overlooked my campus. I always wondered if I'd get up there, then quickly realized it wouldn't happen. Whether I was scooting across the quad to class, leaving the library and heading back to my dorm, rushing to the cafeteria after exercising in the rec center, or scooting toward the shuttles half-drunk, the mountain's majesty was always my backdrop.

Will I ever be atop the mountain to see the QU campus from above, or will I be locked to the land below it? These were the thoughts that plagued me, that reminded me of my disease. Now, for the first time in a long time, surrounded by the forty backs that had just carried my burden, I felt powerful. Free.

CHAPTER 26

Stare at Me

I don't know if the mountain's altitude got to my brain, but things seemed to shift for me after that day. I saw everything more clearly.

I had become comfortable with my disease and comfortable with the special treatment it afforded me. People were kind to me, my professors praised me, and my peers would call me a "savage" or whatever for doing nothing extraordinary at all. Everyone was wicked friendly to me, but I knew after the climb that that would not help me.

On that sunny morning in May, my brothers didn't just carry me up Sleeping Giant. They showed me a better way to the top. It would require me not only to rely on others for help, but to dream big and push myself to get where I needed to go.

People knew me as the friendly boy on the scooter. It was time for me to show everyone I was more than just what their eyes could see. I wasn't just a friendly boy on a scooter but a young man who is bold, charismatic, and hardworking.

For years, people have stared at me—and it's not out of mean-ness. They're just curious about my scooter, my slurred speech, my inward-turning feet, and my "chicken legs." But if people were going to stare, I wanted it to be for better reasons. I didn't want to be gawked at like a car wreck backing up the freeway.

It was time to give people something to *really* stare at—some-thing big, something they wouldn't forget. So the new question I asked myself was, *What would I need to do to keep people staring at me?*

To help everyone see past the scooter, I began taking on more responsibility. I moved into an off-campus, ADA-accessible SigEp house. I lived with Nanna, Mike, and our brother Nick. Even though I had never lived with Nick, he meshed with our trio perfectly. Nick's lovability, loose hips on the dance floor, and desire to always go out of his way to help made him an amazing roommate and friend.

Living off campus might not seem like a big deal for an able-bodied person, but it was in my world. If I fell in my new bedroom or in the shower, I no longer had an RA or twenty floormates there to help. If I wanted dinner, I couldn't go to the cafeteria and grab pre-made food. I had to shop and prepare food on my own. And instead of waking up thirty minutes before class and scooting to my classroom with ten minutes to spare, I had to wake up two hours earlier to get ready, prepare food for the day, drive to campus, then race to class on bunny mode. It was challenging, but I needed this struggle.

Being a political science major, I figured getting some form of government experience would be good. So, I ran to be the president of the Class of 2017. Only members of my class were allowed to vote, and since I knew many students, I liked my chances. But my opponent already had experience as our class president, so he easily beat me. However, unbeknownst to me, if someone runs for president, they are automatically put on the ballot to become a class representative in QU's Student Government Association (SGA). Although I lost the class presidency, I was voted by the 1,800 members of my class to serve as one of eight Class of 2017 representatives. In that position, I worked with various SGA members to address student needs and quality-of-life issues, like adding more food options in the cafeteria, more water stations in the dorms, and more parking spaces for commuters.

The entire student body elected SGA's Executive Board. It featured the president, vice president, vice president for finance, vice president for student experience, and vice president for public relations. These five people were in charge of SGA, and the rest of us followed their command with envy of their power and authority. They all received a stipend, and QU gave them offices on campus. In chess terms, I was an SGA pawn. The SGA president was the king. If an opponent takes the pawn down, it does not affect the game. But a king, queen, bishop, rook, or knight is tougher to knock down. Those positions matter, and I wanted to matter.

As my time as a class representative came to an end, my fraternity brother Jonny asked me to meet him in his office. He'd served on the SGA Executive Board that year and was running unopposed for president. Jonny, a native of Massachusetts with a thick Boston accent, was my "Big" in SigEp—an older brother chosen to be something of a personal mentor to me, on top of being my fraternity brother.

I saw him as a leader, someone I wanted to emulate. Due to his friendly personality and charm, he could have a great conversation with anyone on campus. When he called me to his office, I headed straight there on bunny mode.

Jonny told me he wanted to assemble an ideal Executive Board for the coming year. He asked me to join him as vice president for public relations. The significant duties were fostering a strong relationship between QU and the town QU was in, maintaining a strong image at QU and to QU administrators, and managing an eight-member SGA Public Relations committee featuring representatives from each class. I immediately said yes to Jonny and entered the race against two strong opponents who were campaigning hard. After the entire student body voted, I found out I had won.

On the Executive Board, I now felt like a bishop on the chessboard. I had more authority and influence in the eyes of students, professors, and administrators at QU. I sat in on many meetings with QU administrators about how to better QU's campus, and I met with town officials. I also got to know more students around campus.

During the weekly SGA meetings, each Executive Board member had an opportunity to share updates. As president, Jonny led the meeting, while the four other Executive Board members sat at a table with him and faced the other thirty-seven SGA members.

Those meetings brought me back to my days as a catcher in Little League, looking out at the other players on the field. The experience reminded me of my sports days and the mindset I needed to push myself beyond my limits—Mamba Mentality.

With Jonny's term as president nearing its end, I knew it was time to show the real me, the real Joey.

Having FA has taught me not to squander my time. I try to live in the now. Announcing my candidacy for SGA president required I act now, worry later. I didn't think about how fatigued I became from keeping up with my duties as VP for Public Relations. I didn't think about how I often missed going to the gym for my daily exercise, or how I could barely stay alert without drinking multiple cups of iced coffee per day, or how I overextended myself at times. What would happen if I did win and become the face of the QU student body to every student, parent, alumnus, professor, administrator, and trustee?

No worrying and no whining. Just as if I were back on the court or on the field, I simply wanted to win.

My run for president was no different from how I'd played lacrosse. I was going up against a tough competitor and I needed to go all out. I had to frame pitches, just like in Little League. I held on to concrete causes and goals for the school, among them diversity and accessibility. I was the only person on campus in a scooter. The one student in a wheelchair was graduating. Nobody else knew the physical struggles of a disabled student the way I did. In no particular order, these were some of my complaints:

Too many inaccessible dorms with only steps for entry, forbidding me from visiting my friends.

Zero handicap-accessible parking spots in the sophomore parking lot.

Not being able to get on a shuttle bus.

Academic buildings without automatic doors.

Not knowing if I could get into the cafeteria.

I could implement change.

For my campaign, I leveraged my strong relationships within the Greek system and with administrators with whom I'd worked closely. I wanted to prove I could be president, that the shy kid who scooted around instead of walking was now scooting softly and carrying a big stick.

I ran for president as part of a trio with two of my best friends and fraternity brothers, Alec and George. Alec was running for vice president unopposed, and George was running for VP for finance against one other candidate. Unlike my previous campaign run, this one was exhausting both physically and mentally. Per SGA rules, you can only campaign a week before Election Day. Day after day, I went around campus with George, while Alec promoted our ticket from his computer. We went to the gym, classrooms, and dorms talking with students, hearing out their concerns, and explaining how we would work to improve the school.

"Hello! My name is Joey Mullaney, and I am running to be your next student body president! How can SGA help improve your college experience?"

This question was my opening statement for each of the 600-plus conversations I had that week. I felt like a legit public servant, even ending meetings with hugs before heading to the next campaign post. At night, I focused on campaigning online by creating Instagram and Facebook posts about our ticket's ideas and goals.

When you're in a wheelchair or scooter, many people look at you with pity and sadness. They feel bad for you. They believe your life must be a hundred times harder because you're physically disabled. They might even think you can't do anything impactful because of your disability, or that you're even afraid to go outside.

President Franklin D. Roosevelt famously said, "The only thing we have to fear is fear itself." My fear forced me to stop playing sports in eighth grade. My fear made me stop going to the mall, movie theaters, or anywhere else in public growing up. Sean had to face my fear for me at the assembly as I hid; Petey had to save me from my fear and getting arrested at Rachel's Sweet Sixteen; and Coach Kev had to pardon me from failing because I'd been too afraid to face my fear of public speaking. Even when I thought I'd gotten rid of my fear, my adversary, I was wrong. I'd only distracted myself from facing it head-on. My fear will only end if *I* stop it. I was in control now. I was ready to handle FA.

My running mates and I ran an excellent campaign. I was proud of myself for scooting way outside of my comfort zone. I didn't let my fatigue stop me, I still found time to exercise, and I didn't get upset when I fell while transferring from my scooter to a toilet seat. Instead, I just stayed focused.

No matter the outcome, I'd been amazed by the feeling of seeing my peers stare at me during one of my many stump speeches around campus. The surprised looks on their faces told me they were thinking, *Wow! This kid is for real!*

Finally, Election Day came. I woke up that morning at six and immediately began campaigning online, using texts, social media, and email to tell people to vote. Alec continued our virtual campaign all day, while George and I spent the day continuing to talk with students and encourage them to vote. It almost felt as if my body forgot to get tired because I was continually going on adrenaline. When the polls closed at 8 p.m., the three of us sat together in the cafeteria—my first meal of the day—and waited for the phone call with the results.

At 8:14, I received a call from the man who'd motivated me to strive for greatness. Jonny said, "The results are in! Your opponent received 49.95 percent of the votes, and you received 50.39 percent of the votes. Congratulations, future Mr. Student Body President, you won! All three of you won!"

Here's what I learned about myself: I love hard work. It's a rush for me, and campaigning provided this rush and much more. But I only discovered these things because I had a challenger, and it wasn't my opponent. We all need challengers, even adversaries—any type of force that is trying to stop us, that wants to see us fail. But we don't fail. Instead, we shatter that glass ceiling with grit and hard work.

When I was running for SGA president, people looked past the "guy in the scooter." I didn't receive special treatment. Nobody went easy on me.

After I was announced the winner, I had to put my money where my mouth was. At least I had the summer break to get myself ready.

Senior year. Could time pass this quickly? It seriously felt like yesterday that I arrived on campus. Heading back to QU for my last year was bittersweet. I was excited to begin my presidency, but I couldn't believe it would be the last fall I'd return to campus. My first act as SGA president was to address the freshman class during Welcome Weekend on a stage with QU's executive president, executive vice president, dean of students, and chief marketing officer.

Many thoughts and memories rolled through my head about my freshman year, starting with leaving my twin, second-guessing my decision, learning self-discipline, being scared, falling off my scooter, becoming independent, having great experiences with friends, and rushing SigEp. Now, here I was. QU was my home away from home, and in many ways, I'd discovered my true self there.

I had gone from being petrified about addressing the student body at Lawrence Academy to becoming a pretty damn good speaker, and I had learned to love public speaking despite my physical speech issues. I worked on the Welcome Weekend speech over the summer, writing it twice. Through the process of revising, I developed my voice and my message.

Overlooking the sea of newcomers, some still as young as seventeen, I closed my remarks with:

Before I end, I acknowledge that you will receive a lot of advice in these next few days about what college will be like and how you need to approach these next four years. You've probably been receiving it all summer—from parents, siblings, aunts, uncles, just about anyone who has college stories to share. You do not have to take my advice, because you may think that I do not know the answers since I am only a few years older. However, like your family and friends, I am only trying to help. Here are my three tips:

1. Embrace the change.
2. Step outside your comfort zone.
3. Tackle your fears head-on.

CHAPTER 27

Bunny or Die!

Weeks before my senior year came to a close, I contemplated my life after graduation. I had to make decisions about higher education, job prospects, résumés, internships, money, travel, moving home or moving out, and on and on.

After majoring in political science, did I want to have a career in politics? Would I graduate and begin a master's program or get a job? Would I even have the energy to continue after another year of a forty-hour workweek? Had I chosen the right major? What would it be like to be without my friends? Who would I become beyond QU? What would happen when I got sicker?

The universe invited me to stop my grumblings with a once-in-a-lifetime opportunity to attend the Sixteenth World Summit of Nobel Peace Laureates in Bogotá, Colombia. The trip was organized by the Albert Schweitzer Institute at QU, which conducts various trips year-round to promote education, ethics, and volunteerism. QU could only send fifty students. After an application and an interview, I was selected.

I didn't know much about the Nobel laureates speaking, but I'd always wanted to go abroad and this six-day trip was an excellent time to do it. (Sadly, I wouldn't be in New England for the Super Bowl between the Pats and the Falcons. But the importance of the Super Bowl seemed microscopic compared to this opportunity.)

The event hosted more than 4,500 people from all across the globe, including thousands of college-aged students from various countries. The speakers encouraged all of us to create change for a better world. What they didn't talk about were their degrees, accolades, or salaries. They didn't name-drop, brag, or compete with one another.

I heard from Shirin Ebadi, an Iranian lawyer and human rights defender who founded the Association for the Support of Children's Rights.

And Leymah Gbowee, an activist who organized the peace movement that helped end the second Liberian Civil War in 2003.

And Chaeli Mycroft, a South African ability activist with cerebral palsy who won the International Children's Peace Prize.

And Juan Manuel Santos, former president of Colombia, who worked relentlessly to bring his country's civil war to an end after fifty years.

They all had one thing in common: They'd gone against the odds to do big things. They did so in their own ways and for reasons that had nothing to do with traditional success, fame, fortune, or even a thank you. They did what was right.

Holy crap! That's what I want to do.

I realized it was time for me to impact others and do my part to create a better world. I began to focus on separating the idea of who I thought I was supposed to be from who I knew I was becoming.

When I learned I had FA, the news blindsided me. Even though I was far from alone, I still felt like the only person on the planet. Since that time, the road to self-awareness, confidence, and acceptance has been a bumpy ride. A terminal diagnosis will do that. I might have accomplished a lot so far, but my mental journey will be an ongoing process for the rest of my life. And I understand now that that's perfectly fine.

At first, I wasted a lot of time thinking about how little time I might have. But after Colombia, I decided to take the ticking clock and embrace it while I can. Instead of fighting time, I'm partnering with it.

I am in no way saying I have zero worries about my health. I mean, I simply can't ignore how sick I'm getting. But even though I have physically lost a lot, I've gained much more in purpose and heightened living. To look at my exterior, a stranger on the street might think I'm weak, that I cannot do anything. But I will make sure they see what's on the interior.

"Bunny or Die" has become my mantra. I go full-speed forward. (Not literally, of course, so I don't fall out of my scooter.) No longer do I waste my time hiding or not pursuing all I can.

I want to create a career in which I benefit others. After I graduated from QU, I knew I needed to mature by gaining experience in the world and through education. I wanted to strengthen my skills as a writer and motivational speaker. So, I challenged myself to go to graduate school, write a book, do speaking events, and embrace whatever opportunities—and obstacles—life throws my way.

Thus far:

I earned my master's degree in strategic public relations—with honors!—from Emerson College in Boston.

I lived in Boston in two different apartments.

I learned to take the crowded T around Boston's surrounding neighborhoods and navigate my scooter through Boston's busy streets, all on my own.

I tried to become an elite Adaptive CrossFit Athlete but failed miserably. *Glad I tried.*

I gave motivational speeches at awards banquets, schools, libraries, and more. And in doing so, I let people see the real me.

I wrestled a grizzly bear. ;)

I started a website and a blog.

I finished my memoir in my mid-twenties, during a global pandemic. (And I learned how to wear a mask properly!)

What's next on my to-do list?

I'm not quite sure yet. But whatever it is, you can be certain I'll be doing it on bunny mode.

ACKNOWLEDGMENTS

I would not be where I am today without the continuous support I've received from my whole family, especially my immediate family. During good times and bad, I was never alone. You all saw the potential in me and stayed by me. Thank you, fam.

To my sister, Kaela, thank you for paving the way for me through the unknowns. I am forever grateful.

My friends, I love you all. I would have hidden in my playroom from age thirteen to the present day if you weren't in my life. For friendships formed in preschool and up through graduate school, I thank you.

To my writing partner, Michele Matrisciani, you are the best. I began working with you a month after my four years at Quinnipiac University ended. Since that time, you have been nothing short of perfect. Whether it was teaching me how to write a memoir, revising my work, shopping around my book proposal, or editing my manuscript, you stuck with me. You worked tirelessly to make my dream of writing this book come true. You are amazing, Michele! Thank you.

I would like to thank KiCam Projects for believing in me and allowing me to write this. I would also like to thank Jennifer Scroggins from KiCam Projects for directly working with me, helping me, and guiding me throughout this process.

I've been religiously working out since I was eighteen years old with my trainer, Nick Normandin, who is like family now. I am grateful to have Nick in my life. His continuous support has shown me I can do so much more than I ever knew.

Leominster, we've had our ups and downs, but you're the only town in the world that I can call my hometown. For that, I am forever thankful.

Thank you to St. Anna Catholic School, Lawrence Academy, Quinnipiac University, and Emerson College for everything. And thank you to all my teachers and professors from those schools. You have all helped shape my life and have developed me into becoming a well-educated person.

Thank you to Sigma Phi Epsilon, especially SigEp at Quinnipiac University. The men I met during my time at QU are some of the most remarkable people I have ever known. I will never be able to truly convey my love and appreciation for you, boys. Just know, I will always care about you guys. *Purple and Red 'til the day I'm dead!*

Thank you to everyone out there who has helped me get to where I am today. We did it.

One Love,
Joey

About the Author

 Joey Mullaney helps young adults and teens make the most of their lives, no matter what obstacles they face. Diagnosed as a child with a terminal, degenerative disease called Friedreich's ataxia, Joey began a long, bumpy ride to self-awareness, confidence, and acceptance. His triumphs have been documented on *Good Morning America* and in *USA Today* and have gone viral on YouTube. Now twenty-six, Joey is an inspirational speaker and writer who blogs at joeymullaney.com. In person or on the page, Joey provides his audience with a humorous, uplifting, and motivational punch in the arm.